GW00367829

California

by Richard Minnich

Richard Minnich comes from a long line of serious travelers. Bitten by the travel bug at an early age, he is fortunate to have seen a good bit of the world. To him, writing about his travels is fulfilling and a welcome diversion to his life as a writer/producer of theater and film. Essential *California* is his first guidebook. Originally from Pennsylvania, he currently resides in Los Angeles.

Above: *Mural at Venice Beach*

AA Publishing

Frog Jumping Jubilee, Angel's Camp

Written by Richard Minnich
Updated by Julie Jares

Reprinted Nov 1998; Reprinted Apr 1999
Reprinted May 2001
Reprinted 2004. Information verified and updated.
Reprinted Aug 2004
Reprinted 2006. Information updated and verified.
Reprinted Feb 2007

© Automobile Association Developments Limited 2006

Published by AA Publishing, a trading name of Automobile Association Developments Limited, whose registered office is Fanum House, Basing View, Basingstoke, Hampshire RG21 4EA. Registered number 1878835.

The Automobile Association retains the copyright in the original edition © 1998 and in all subsequent editions, reprints and amendments.

A CIP catalogue record for this book is available from the British Library.

All rights reserved. No part of this publication may be reproduced, stored in a retrieval system, or transmitted in any form or by any means—electronic, photocopying, recording or otherwise—unless the written permission of the publishers has been obtained beforehand. This book may not be sold, resold, hired out or otherwise disposed of by way of trade in any form of binding or cover other than that in which it is published, without the prior consent of the publisher.

The contents of this publication are believed correct at the time of printing. Nevertheless, AA Publishing accept no responsibility for errors, omissions or changes in the details given, or for the consequences of readers' reliance on this information. This does not affect your statutory rights. Assessments of attractions, hotels and restaurants are based upon the author's own experience and contain subjective opinions that may not reflect the publisher's opinion or a reader's experience. We have tried to ensure accuracy, but things do change, so please let us know if you have any comments or corrections.

A03309

Colour separation: Keenes, Andover
Printed and bound in Italy by Printers Trento srl

Find out more about AA Publishing and the wide range of travel publications and services the AA provides by visiting our website at www.theAA.com/travel

Contents

About this Book

KEY TO SYMBOLS

- map reference to the maps found in the What to See section (see below)
- address or location
- telephone number
- opening times
- restaurant or café on premises or nearby
- nearest underground train station
- nearest bus/tram route
- nearest overground train station
- ferry crossings and excursions by boat
- travel by air
- tourist information
- facilities for visitors with disabilities
- admission charge
- other places of interest nearby
- other practical information
- ➤ indicates the page where you will find a fuller description

This book is divided into five sections to cover the most important aspects of your visit to California.

Viewing California pages 5–14
An introduction to California by the author
California's Features
Essence of California
The Shaping of California
Peace and Quiet
California's Famous

Top Ten pages 15–26
The author's choice of the Top Ten places to see in California, each with practical information.

What to See pages 27–90
The four main areas of California, each with its own brief introduction and an alphabetical listing of the main attractions.
Practical information
Snippets of "Did You Know..." information
4 suggested walks
4 suggested tours
2 features

Where To... pages 91–116
Detailed listings of the best places to eat, stay, shop, take the children and be entertained.

Practical Matters pages 117–24
A highly visual section containing essential travel information.

Maps
All map references are to the individual maps found in the What to See section of this guide.
For example, Alcatraz has the reference 29D6—indicating the page on which the map is located and the grid square in which the island is to be found. A list of the maps that have been used in this travel guide can be found in the index.

Prices
Where appropriate, an indication of the cost of an establishment is given by **$** signs:
$$$** denotes higher prices, **$$** denotes average prices, while **$ denotes lower charges.

Star Ratings
Most of the places described in this book have been given a separate rating:

✪✪✪ Do not miss
✪✪ Highly recommended
✪ Worth seeing

Viewing California

Above: *Sculpture on Rodeo Drive, Los Angeles*

Richard Minnich's California

Describing California and its people is like trying to describe a beautiful painting: most people will have a different perspective and feeling. The word that most readily comes to mind is *extreme*. Nowhere on earth can one find such extreme variances of scenic splendor or inhabitants. Within an 80-mile (129km) span are the highest and lowest elevations in the United States, each with its own unique beauty.

From the very first person to set foot in the state to its most recent émigré, the trait that has most greatly characterized the state's populace is a deep commitment to adventure. California seems to define the concept of diversity with both its geography and inhabitants. With nearly every culture represented throughout the state, there are enough dining and entertainment selections to suit everyone's desire.

The Living Desert, a 1,200-acre (486-ha) garden and wild animal park in Palm Desert

California offers virtually every type of terrain, from desert to ocean to mountain, and environments ranging from small farming communities to giant metropolises that teem with cultural activity 24 hours a day.

If you're simply looking for rest and recuperation on your vacation, this is the place to visit. California is the epitome of "laid back," even in its busiest cities. At the same time the state is the nation's leader for fashion and fun.

So often when traveling, one's preconceived notion of a destination and the reality of that destination vary greatly. But whatever your most romantic visions of California might be, rest assured your visit to this kaleidoscopic state will not disappoint. It is almost impossible to overestimate the grandeur that awaits.

California's Features

Geography

- Population: 35,500,000.
- Land area: 155,959sq miles (399,894sq km).
- Highest point: Mount Whitney (14,494ft/4,419m).
- Lowest point: Death Valley (282ft/86m below sea level).
- Capital: Sacramento.

Economic Factors

- California is the leading agricultural economy in the US, primarily because of its fruit crops: prunes, oranges, grapes, peaches, apricots, figs, lemons, avocados, dates, nectarines and rice plums. Other agriculture products include cotton, walnuts, almonds, sugar beet, tomatoes, eggs, turkeys, sunflowers and honey.
- Napa and Sonoma valleys (➤ 88) are famous for their wineries. Southern California has both film and television production and manufactures military aircraft and missiles.

Sports and Leisure

- Almost every conceivable sport, from boating and other watersports to sky-diving and rollerblading.

Animal Life

- The Pacific Ocean is home to humpback whales, sea otters, seals, sea lions, dolphins, elephant seals, and blue whales, the largest mammals in the world, as well as hundreds of species of smaller fish. The pupfish (desert sardine) has even managed to survive in arid Death Valley (➤ 71).
- Land animals include bison, deer, Roosevelt elk, mountain goats, big-horn sheep, mountain lions, bobcats, wild burros and black bear.
- Desert creatures include iguanas, chuckawallas, pronghorn antelope, coyotes, kangaroo rats and various insects and reptiles, including the dangerous black widow spider and the poisonous rattlesnake.
- Birdlife ranges from the exotic white-faced ibis and the tiny hummingbird to the bald and golden eagle and the mundane sea gull.

Plants

- Unique trees in California are the eucalyptus, sequoias, redwoods, Joshua trees and many varieties of palm. Various cacti and flowers also abound year-round.

Climate

California is known for its diversity of climates. Generally speaking, the south is warmer and the north cooler. The bay areas are renowned for their fog. The mountainous areas are known for pleasant summers and snowy winters at the higher elevations. The San Joaquin and Sacramento valleys are extremely hot during the summer months and cool and foggy the rest of the year. As a rule, most parts of the state are cool in the evenings.

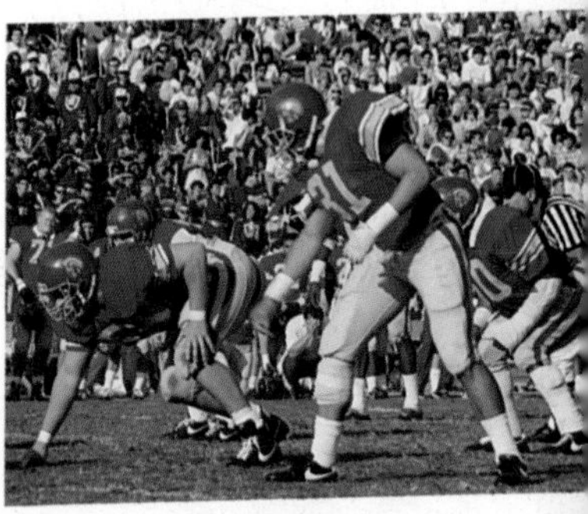

USC Trojans in the Coliseum

Essence of California

One of the best things about California is that you rarely have to plan your vacation around the seasons. If you wish to relax on the beach, accommodations range from luxurious oceanside resorts to basic camping facilities. If you want continuous entertainment, the state abounds with theme parks, fairs and festivals.

For the explorer or seeker of beauty, the natural habitat is varied and unbeatable. For a tour of the coastline, the Amtrak rail system runs from the top to the bottom of the state and features plush, picture-windowed lounge cars. The landscape is great for the photographer.

Bottom: *Zabriskie Point, Death Valley National Monument*

THE 10 ESSENTIALS

If you only have a short time to visit California, or would like to get a really complete picture of the state, here are the essentials:

- **Take a drive (or train)** along California's famous Route 1 for fantastic ocean views to the west and spectacular rolling hills or majestic mountain ranges to the east.
- **Spend the day** at one of the many beaches. Surf, sun or rent a bicycle, boogieboard or rollerblades.
- **Walk across the Golden Gate Bridge** (➤ 19) from San Francisco to Marin County. Spend an hour or so wandering around the small towns on the other side, then you can either walk or hop on a ferry back to San Francisco. Finish the day with a cable-car ride to view the city's marvellous architecture.
- **Spend a day hiking or backpacking** in one of the many national or state parks. The Joshua Tree National Monument is an especially good one (➤ 73).
- **Experience the excitement** of professional sports in San Francisco, San Diego or Los Angeles or attend a horse race at one of the major tracks.
- **Go window-shopping** along Beverly Hill's exclusive Rodeo Drive (➤ 48, 49) or El Paseo Drive in Palm Springs (➤ 107).
- **Take a drive through the Napa Valley** wine country, stopping at any of the wineries for a tour and some wine-tasting (➤ 88). This is also an excellent place to buy your souvenirs to take back home.
- **Visit a theme park.** Disneyland is the most well-known (➤ 18), but Balboa Park/San Diego Zoo is exciting too (➤ 16).
- **Take the one-day cruise** from San Pedro or Newport Beach across to Catalina Island (➤ 17).
- **Tour one of Hollywood's** motion picture studios for an inside look at the making of screen magic. Universal Studios (➤ 54) is the most famous.

Above: *Universal Studios*
Below: *Characters from Sea World, San Diego*

The Shaping of California

***c*7,000BC**
La Brea Tar Pit woman, first known LA resident, dies mysteriously.

AD1542
Juan Cabrillo enters "the Bay of Smokes" (San Pedro Bay).

1579
Sir Francis Drake claims San Francisco Bay area for Queen Elizabeth I.

1769
Franciscan monk Junípero Serra founds Mission San Diego de Alcala.

1777
Monterey becomes capital of Spanish-controlled California.

1781
Pueblo de Los Angeles is founded by 44 settlers of European, African and Native American heritages.

1790
Los Angeles population reaches 139.

1821
Spain grants independence to California.

1846
President Polk tries to purchase California (including parts of the present-day New Mexico) from Mexico for $40 million. Mexican-American War begins; US flag raised in San Francisco and Los Angeles.

1847
Yerba Buena, whose population is just a few hundred, is renamed San Francisco.

1848
James Wilson Marshall discovers gold at Coloma.

1849
Gold Rush attracts over 300,000 prospectors. San Jose becomes state capital.

1850
California joins the US as its 31st state.

1853
Levi Strauss creates denim jeans in San Francisco; Don Matteo Keller plants the state's first orange trees.

1854
Sacramento becomes the state capital.

1857
Fort Tejon earthquake (8.0) rocks Los Angeles.

1858
Wine industry is born.

1862
Telegraph connects San Francisco and New York.

1869
Railroad joins the east and west coasts.

1873
First cable-car in San Francisco. University of California established at Berkeley.

1881
First *Los Angeles Times* rolls off the presses. First snowfall in down-town LA.

The San Francisco earthquake of 1906

1882
First LA telephone directory is a mere three pages long.

1906
Earthquake and fire levels most of San Francisco.

1907
George Feeth introduces surfing to Southern California.

1908
Colonel William Selig opens first Hollywood film studio to produce *In the Sultan's Power.*

1915
Telephone connects New York and San Francisco.

1927
Charles Lindbergh's *The Spirit of St. Louis* is built by Ryan Airlines in San Diego.

1929
First Academy Awards presentation at the Hollywood Roosevelt Hotel.

1933
Donald Douglas builds first mass-produced commercial aircraft, the DC-2, at Santa Monica.

1935
Statewide irrigation system turns the arid central valley plains into a lush green oasis.

1936
San Francisco-Oakland Bay Bridge opens.

1937
Golden Gate Bridge opens.

1940
First western freeway, Arroyo Seco Parkway, opens in LA.

1942
Japanese shell Santa Barbara.

1945
United Nations signs charter in San Francisco.

1947
Anti-Communist hearings lead to Hollywood black-listing.

Marilyn Monroe

1955
Disneyland opens.

1962
California becomes the most populous state in America.

1963
Marilyn Monroe dies.

1964
Beatles play Hollywood Bowl.

1968
Senator Robert Kennedy assassinated at LA's Ambassador Hotel.

1977
Silicon Valley develops Apple II, first market-able personal computer.

1980
Ronald Reagan, actor and ex-California Governor becomes US president.

1984
California hosts Summer Olympics.

1989
Earthquake (7.1) shakes San Francisco.

1992
Worst rioting in American history in Los Angeles after verdict in the police-beating trial of Rodney King.

1995
Jury acquits O. J. Simpson for the murders of Nicole Brown Simpson and Ronald Goldman.

1998–2000
California celebrates 150 years since the discovery of gold, the gold rush and the state's creation.

2003
Actor Arnold Schwarzenegger becomes California's 38th governor in a controversial recall election.

Peace & Quiet

Rarely can you visit an area and have so many options to choose from to amuse and entertain yourself, but in California there are also as many choices that offer nothing but relaxation and reflection in tranquil surroundings.

Southern California

Separate from the mainland, the picturesque Channel Islands National Park and Catalina Island (➤ 17) provide a respite from the hustle and bustle of the city. Biking and horseback riding are offered on the islands, and both are wonderful for hiking.

Back on the mainland, in Santa Monica Mountains National Recreation Area hiking trails abound, and the coastline views are incredible from Sandstone Peak, its highest elevation at 3,111ft (948m). Nearby Point Dume is a popular secluded beach great for winter-time whale-watching. For nature at its best, visit the undeveloped Crystal Cove State Park near Laguna Beach and Torrey Pines State Reserve near La Jolla, in San Diego.

If you enjoy the desert, Anza-Borrego Desert State Park (➤ 82) and Lost Palm Oasis in Joshua Tree National Monument (➤ 73) provide incredible hiking and camping. As the ocean calms with its cascading sound and magnetic emanations, the desert soothes with unremitting sun and vast stillness. The extreme heat and dryness attract numerous birds, mammals and reptiles as well as intriguing plant life. Campgrounds are scattered throughout, many amid great climbing rocks, if you tire of merely sitting.

Rock-climbers are often seen scaling the smooth granite boulders at Joshua Tree National Monument

Central California

Gaviota State Park, Refugio State Beach and El Capitan State Beach, all in Santa Barbara County, offer perfect alternatives to the more crowded outdoor areas. After some quiet time on the beach, explore the hills and hiking trails just a short distance away.

Near Carmel, the Point Lobos State Reserve offers spectacular views of the Monterey cypress. Relax in the sun or take a more strenuous 50-mile (81-km) bicycle ride through the Carmel Valley.

Northern California

If you like to hike, head for the Lost Coast Trail in Humboldt County. Just south of Eureka, the King Range National Conservation Area is a favorite with back-packers. Coastal redwoods and Roosevelt elk can be seen in abundance in the Prairie Creek Redwoods State Park. In the Shasta area, the Trinity Alps Wilderness offers great trails, or if you'd rather ride, there are exotic llamas for hire. In the Sierra Nevadas, the best hiking is in the aptly named Desolation Wilderness near Lake Tahoe (➤ 75).

Rock-climbers swear that scaling the granite face of such towering spires as El Capitan and Half Dome, in Yosemite National Park (➤ 26), is both invigorating and relaxing at the same time.

Gardens

If you don't want to leave the metropolitan areas, you can still escape by visiting one of the many botanical gardens in the state. The Self-Realization Centers in both Los Angeles and San Diego provide peaceful gardens in which to meditate. One little-known area is the Greystone estate (now a park) just off Doheny Drive, above Sunset in Los Angeles. The Asian temples of the major cities are also quiet spots, and many are surrounded by beautiful Zen gardens.

Stowe Lake, Golden Gate National Park

The Beach

Take some time out to experience the beach side of the Golden State. Nap on one of the many strands, or better yet, spend a night or two at a beachside hotel. Let the roar of the Pacific Ocean drown out civilization's daily annoyances and the sun recharge your solar batteries. Add to this the gentle sea breezes through your hair, and the refreshing feel of salt water on your body.

California's Famous

One of Hollywood's most famous sons: John Wayne

Film and Television

Hollywood has created hundreds of celebrities, from Marilyn Monroe to John Wayne. Directors Francis Ford Coppola and George Lucas, of *American Graffiti* and *Star Wars* fame respectively, are both Northern Californians who have set a standard for excellence in the film industry.

Music

Jerry Garcia, leader of the Grateful Dead, inspired the San Francisco music scene of the 1960s, which rocketed such musicians as Janis Joplin and The Jefferson Airplane to stardom. Jim Morrison, poet and singer for the Doors, was a student at UCLA film school and is considered one of the great musicians to emerge from Southern California. And you can't mention California music without including the Beach Boys, who captured Southern California's surf lifestyle with their music.

Literature

Dashiell Hammett, author of *The Maltese Falcon*, was a native Californian, and Beat Generation hero Jack Kerouac claimed San Francisco as his adult home (➤ 38). Jack London hails from Glen Ellen in Sonoma Valley (➤ 88), and John Steinbeck was born in Salinas (➤ 85).

Explorers

John Muir, founder of the Sierra Club, considered California paradise, and 1856 presidential candidate John C. Fremont understandably preferred exploring California to politics. Who wouldn't?

Politics

Two 20th-century US presidents emerged from the state: Richard Nixon and Ronald Reagan. Nixon is remembered for his scandal-caused resignation and Reagan was the first actor elected to the highest office in the nation.

Business

Media mogul William Randolph Hearst (➤ 20), E. W. Scripps, founder of United Press International, and Orville Redenbacher, the popcorn king, all hail from the state.

Scandal
Author/humorists Artemus Ward, Bret Harte, Mark Twain, Ambrose Bierce and Joaquin Miller hung out together in 1860s San Francisco. Their friend, Adah Menken, scandalized the city by appearing in Byron's *Mazeppa* wearing nothing but a flesh-colored body suit. She was strapped backwards on a horse as it galloped up a three-story stage mountain complete with waterfalls and chasms.

Top Ten

Above: *Parking on Rodeo Drive*

1
Balboa Park

This immense expanse of parks and museums includes the world-renowned San Diego Zoo.

Balboa Park, the pride of San Diego

A 100-tone chime serenades from the 200-ft (61-m) California Tower, creating an exquisite backdrop for the historical buildings, museums and gardens of this 1,200-acre (486-ha) park. Start your visit from the main thoroughfare, El Prado (The Promenade). Here you'll find original exhibit halls from the 1915 Panama–California International Exposition, most notably the Casa del Prado. The Timken Museum of Art, a few blocks south, has interesting Russian icons among its exhibits.

At the park's center are several small museums: San Diego History Museum, Museum of Photographic Arts, Model Railroad Museum and Hall of Champions (sports). The nearby Reuben H. Fleet Space Theater and Science Center provides hands-on exhibits for youngsters. The Natural History Museum features exhibits of southwest desert and marine life, and at the end of the plaza are The Museum of Man (➤ 61) and the San Diego Museum of Art.

Visit any of the three stages of the Globe Theatre to see contemporary or Shakespearean plays, or enjoy a summer musical at The Starlight Bowl.

Simply stated, the **San Diego Zoo** (➤ 111 for practical information) is among the finest zoos in the world. The 100 acres (40ha) simulate the natural habitats of the 800 species living here, and allows expansive roaming of its 4,000 animals, which include the only pair of pandas in the US. The Children's Zoo offers close-up views. There are guided bus tours, as well as an aerial tramway that rises 170ft (52m) over the zoo's grottoes and mesas, providing a fine overview of the park.

- 59B2
- 1 mile (1.61km) north of downtown San Diego
- 619/239 0512
- Daily 9–4.30 (4 in winter)
- Restaurants, stands ($$)
- 7, 7A or 7B from downtown
- Excellent
- Moderate
- Visitor Center sells multi-day passports to the park; free in-park tram

2

Catalina Island

Known as "The Island of Romance," Santa Catalina Island is a perfect blend of relaxed resort, pristine shoreline and untouched wilderness.

Discovered in 1542 by Juan Rodriguez Cabrillo, Santa Catalina (commonly called Catalina Island) is roughly 26 miles (42km) from the mainland. One of the eight California Channel Islands, it is 21 miles (34km) long and 8 miles (13km) wide. No cars are allowed on the island, so use the public transportation or rent the electric golf carts and bicycles available.

In 1811, the indigenous Gabrileño Indians were forced to resettle on the mainland, leaving the island that later became the private property of the Wrigley family, the chewing gum heirs. Today, 86 percent of the island is owned by the non-profit Santa Catalina Island Conservancy, established in 1972 to preserve the island's natural beauty. The island provides a welcome retreat from mainland crowds, with its silent beaches, water sports, picturesque pier and deep-sea fishing.

The 1929 Avalon Casino is the most famous building on the island, best known for its art deco ballroom, which in its heyday was host to many of the world's most famous orchestras and big bands. The Catalina Island Museum, on the first floor of the Casino, exhibits the island's history. The Wrigley Mansion, with its botanical gardens, and the Avalon Pier, in the middle of Avalon Bay, provide fine views of the interior hills and the breathtaking shoreline.

69D1

Visitors Center, Green Pier

310/510 1520

Daily 8–5

Restaurants ($$$)

Catalina Express 310/519 1212 or 800/618 5533; 1 hour each way; hourly from San Pedro or Long Beach.
Catalina Passenger Service 949/673 5245; 75 minutes each way; departs from Balboa Pavilion 9, returns 4.30

Helicopter Service from Island Express 800/228 2566; 15 minutes each way

Travel moderate; exhibits inexpensive

Cruise ship at Catalina Island

3
Disneyland Park

Disneyland sets the standard for theme parks. This "happiest place on earth" attracts 12 million visitors each year.

Children and adults alike are enchanted by the illusion and entertainment of "magic kingdom," opened in 1955. The 80-acre (32-ha) park is divided into eight sections, offering such diverse attractions as fantasy rides, musical performances, parades, restaurants and shops.

The turrets and spires of Sleeping Beauty Castle

© Disney Enterprises, Inc.

69D1

1313 Harbor Boulevard, Anaheim

714/781 4565

Summer Mon–Fri 9am–midnight (until 1am Sat); winter Mon–Fri 10–6 (until 9pm weekends, hols). Hours can vary, check first

Very good; free strollers and wheelchairs

Expensive

Hours and prices subject to change; on busy days park at the Disneyland Hotel and ride the monorail to the park

A series of pastel-colored walkways lead from the central plaza at the end of Main Street, U.S.A. into the various themed areas, each with their own attractions. Mickey's Toontown brings out the kid in everyone; Adventureland offers a jungle boat ride and the charming "Tiki Room". New Orleans Square has a Mississippi steamwheeler, the "Pirates of the Caribbean" attraction and the "Haunted Mansion."

In Frontierland, you can careen down Big Thunder Mountain Railroad on a runaway train or raft across to Tom Sawyer Island. Critter Country is the home of the "Splash Mountain" flume ride. Fantasyland begins when you cross the moat to Sleeping Beauty Castle, while Tomorrowland explores the future with attractions like "Space Mountain" and "Star Tours." For the courageous, the "Indiana Jones Adventure" takes you on a trek to the Temple of the Forbidden Eye. Disney characters roam the streets and pose for pictures. California Adventure Park, a celebration of the State's past and future, is next to Disneyland.

4

Golden Gate Bridge & National Recreation Area

The Golden Gate Bridge is quite easily the most beautiful and easily recognized bridge in the world.

The rust-colored symbol of the West Coast stands as a beacon at the entrance of San Francisco Bay. Built in 1937 it is beautiful and impressive from any angle. Often cloaked in fog, the bridge is extraordinarily graceful and delicate in design even though its overall length is 8,981ft (2,737m) and the stolid towers reach 746ft (227m) high. Connecting San Francisco to Marin County and northern California, the suspension bridge withstands winds of up to 100mph (161kph) and swings as much as 27ft (8m). Enjoy the drive over, or walk across for a truly spectacular perspective.

Golden Gate Park, the largest urban national park in the US, covers 74,000 acres (29,959ha) from San Mateo County to Tomales Bay. The giant recreation area offers many attractions, including Fort Mason on San Francisco's waterfront. A former military embarkation point for soldiers during World War II, today the fort is the site of museums, theaters, galleries, restaurants and the last unaltered, operational liberty ship, the SS *Jeremiah O'Brien*.

The Golden Gate Promenade is a scenic bayshore hike stretching 3.5 miles (5.5km) from Hyde Street Pier to Fort Point and beyond, across the Golden Gate Bridge. Among other sights in this impressive area are The Presidio, Baker Beach, Cliff House, Ocean Beach and Fort Funston, most of which are accessible by San Francisco's MUNI system.

28B5

Golden Gate Bridge

MUNI 28; 415/554 6999 (hotline)

Excellent

Free northbound; southbound toll inexpensive

Alcatraz tour info 415/705 5555

Recreation Area

GGNRA, Building 201, Fort Mason, San Francisco, CA 94123

415/561 4700 (information line)

Mon–Fri 9.30–4.30

Cafés, stands ($)

Excellent

Moderate

Instantly recognizable—Golden Gate Bridge

5
Hearst Castle

68C2

750 Hearst Castle Road, San Simeon

805/927 2020 or 800/444 4445

Daily 8.20–3.20 (Dec start times may vary). Five different tours offered daily

Excellent

Moderate

214 miles (345km) southeast of San Francisco; 242 miles (390km) northwest of Los Angeles; parking just off Hwy 1 with shuttles buses to the castle. Four tours, priced separately. Tour 1 is recommended for first-time visitors. Reservations suggested

A rich man's castle—William Hearst's dream come true

William Randolph Hearst's tribute to excess and grandiosity crowns a hillside above the village of San Simeon.

The history of this fabulous castle dates back to 1865, when George Hearst purchased 40,000 acres (16,194ha) of Mexican land adjacent to San Simeon Bay. His son, newspaper magnate William Randolph, began the castle when he took possession of the land in 1919, which now numbers 250,000 acres (101,215ha). Using steamers and chain-driven trucks to transport materials to the remote spot, the palatial residence was not completed until 1947.

Casa Grande, as the mammoth mansion is called, boasts more than 100 rooms filled with priceless objects of art and antiques. It is one of seven estates owned by William Randolph, and was donated to the California Park Service in 1957.

Among the mansion's unique attributes are gothic fireplaces, Renaissance paintings (displayed in one of the 19 sitting rooms) and ceilings ranging in style from 16th-century Spanish to 18th-century Italian. In its prime, the doge's suite was reserved for the most important guests: presidents, visiting heads of state such as Winston Churchill and Hollywood luminaries. Marble colonnades and statuary flanking the indoor and outdoor pools replicate figures of antiquity.

There are also five greenhouses with over 700,000 annuals providing year-round color, tennis courts and a movie theater (in which Walt Disney hosted the first screening of *Snow White* in 1938). There are also two libraries, riding stables and the world's largest private zoo.

6
Hollywood

A one-time cow town, Hollywood is now the movie-making capital of the world and trend-setting center of glamour, glitter and excess.

The name that has drawn many a starry-eyed hopeful

Hollywood Boulevard is a relatively short street, but is one of the best known of all Los Angeles thoroughfares. Its wealth of art deco architecture has elevated it to the status of national historic district. From the 1920s to the 1950s, Hollywood boasted some of the country's largest movie palaces and exclusive department stores. As the movie industry expanded outward, Hollywood lost its luster, but the faded star is now staging a comeback.

The Hollywood Roosevelt Hotel (➤ 101), site of the first Academy Awards, has been renovated and displays historical film memorabilia throughout. An ambitious three-block redevelopment project around Sid Grauman's 1927 Chinese Theatre (now Mann's Chinese) offers shops, cinemas, restaurants and the Hollywood Studio Museum.

Hollywood abounds with guided bus tours of every sort. Walking tours of its bronze-starred Walk of Fame are extremely popular. Begun in 1960 with only eight stars, there are now close to 3,000 celebrity prints. The 1920s Hollywood sign can best be viewed by venturing up Beachwood Canyon on the eastern edge of Hollywood or from Griffith Observatory, high atop Mount Hollywood.

Paramount Studio provides a peek into the world of film-making. Free tickets to several popular TV shows are readily available outside Mann's Theatre or through the major network studios.

Hawkers along Sunset and Hollywood Boulevards offer surprisingly accurate maps to celebrity homes at a low price; you can drive yourself or take a bus tour.

 46B4

Hollywood Visitors Bureau, 333 South Hope Street

213/624 7300; 323/937 3661 (LA TOURS); 323/469 8311 (Hollywood Chamber of Commerce)

 Numerous restaurants, some open 24 hours ($–$$$)

7
Monterey Peninsula

68B3

122 miles (197km) southeast of San Francisco; 334 miles (539km) northwest of LA

831/649 1770 (Visitors Bureau); 831/649 7118 (State Historical Park); 831/624 2522 (Carmel Business Association); 831/659 0333 (Steinbeck Country Tours)

Various restaurants ($–$$$)

Monterey–Salinas Transit

Inexpensive

"This is the California men dreamed of years ago. The face of the earth as the Creator intended it to look." Henry Miller

For more than 300 years the Monterey Peninsula has enchanted everyone who has seen it. Formed by the Monterey and Carmel bays, the peninsula juts into the Pacific Ocean 120 miles (194km) south of San Francisco. Pristine beaches, craggy rock formations and wind- and wave-warped cypresses make the area among the most popular scenic spots in the world.

Nowhere in California is the state's Latin heritage more prevalent than in Monterey, where its exquisitely restored adobe buildings give testimony to the Spanish and Mexican periods of California history.

From art galleries in Carmel (➤ 71) to the grand estates in the dense woods of the Del Monte Forest, the scenic 17-Mile Drive through the forest between Pacific Grove and Carmel is almost incomparable in beauty.

The legacy of famed California author John Steinbeck can be traced at The National Steinbeck Center in Salinas (open daily). You can also visit his preserved cottage in nearby Pacific Grove.

Monterey Beach

Carmel-by-the-Sea is an enchanting village. Much of its architecture is reminiscent of rural European and early California styles. Monterey's Fisherman's Wharf has a magnificent promenade of fish markets, shops and theaters. For a different perspective, a sail can be arranged aboard the restored tall ship *Californian*.

Established at the turn of the century by a group of writers and artists, Carmel was originally a planned resort. As its popularity soared, it took on the reputation of something completely different: an exclusive bohemian retreat. Resisting efforts for modernization, Carmel has preserved its idyllic setting. At Point Lobos State Reserve, 2 miles (3.5km) south of Carmel, harbor seals, gray whales and California sea lions frolic among a variety of sea birds and pelicans, a sight seen nowhere else in the world.

Sea lions are a familiar sight at Monterey

8
Napa Valley

Only 30 miles (48km) long and 3 miles (5km) across at its widest, this little valley boasts some 220 wineries.

Yountville, in the Napa Valley, is an important center of wine production

68B4

Visitor Information Center, 1310 Napa Town Center, Napa, 94559

707/226 7459 (Visitor Information Center) 707/253 2111; 800/427 4124 (Napa Valley Wine Train)

Hours vary; some tours require reservations

Restaurants in the towns ($$–$$$)

Free–inexpensive

Leader of the American wine industry, the Napa Valley boasts such well-known names as Robert Mondavi, Domaine Chandon, Beringer and Sterling. Although the greatest concentration of wineries is along State Route 29, north from Napa to Calistoga, knowledgeable travelers use the Silverado Trail, a scenic, vineyard-lined parallel road along the eastern edge of the valley.

The city of Napa is the largest, although each of the valley towns has its charms. In Calistoga there are spas and geysers, one of which shoots 60ft (18m) into the air every 40 minutes. St. Helena claims many of the region's best dining and lodging choices, as well as a wine library and the Silverado Museum. An ancient volcanic eruption from Washington's Mount St. Helens around 3 million years ago caused the giant redwoods of California to become instantly petrified. You'll find the Petrified Forest between Calistoga and Santa Rosa.

Outside of these towns lie more wineries, markets, inns, quiet picnic areas and historic parklands. Most visitors tour the vineyards, which offer a look at the wine-making process and feature wine-tastings, but there are also five different walking tours of the incredible architectural highlights of the valley (maps available at the information center). If possible, avoid the crowded summer weekends. Most vintners now charge a small fee for the tastings and a few require reservations.

9
Redwood National Park

A vast forest of giant redwoods grows naturally nowhere else in the country except in this coastal region.

68B6

National Park Headquarters, 1111 Second Street, Crescent City, 95531

707/464 6101 (Redwood National Park Information Center)

Restaurants ($); picnic facilities

Moderate

Before California's famous gold rush, and the resulting surge of new population, the world's tallest trees blanketed an area 30 miles (48km) wide and 450 miles (726km) long. The majority of today's redwood "stands" are along US 101, from Leggett north to Crescent City. It is about a five-hour drive from San Francisco to the southern edge of the Redwood Forest, via the scenic coastal highway.

A small segment of old growth redwoods and outstanding coastal scenery have been protected in the 106,000-acre (42,915-ha) Redwood National Park. Eight miles (13km) of shoreline roads and more than 150 miles (242km) of trails afford close-up encounters with these trees and the abundant plant and animal life they nurture.

Giant redwood—one of the world's largest trees

The three main state parks within the Park's boundaries are Prairie Creek, Del Norte Coast and Jedediah Smith. Campers favor Prairie Creek because of its herds of native Roosevelt elk and great expansive beach (Gold Bluffs Beach). Lady Bird Johnson Cove is especially beautiful. Don't miss the Libby Tree, the tallest known tree, which towers to over 368ft (112m).

A drive through Del Norte Coast park allows you to enjoy spectacular ocean views and the inland forest simultaneously. The giant redwoods grow closest to the shoreline at the Damnation Creek Trail. In the spring, this area is the best place to view the abundant growth of rhododendrons and azaleas.

At the north end of the park, the Jedediah Smith terrain gives you an elevated perspective.

10
Yosemite National Park

 69D4

Yosemite Valley Visitors Center

 209/372 0200

Apr–end May 9–6; Jul–end Aug 8–8; Sep–end Oct 8–6; Nov–end Mar 9–5

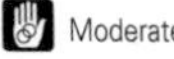 Restaurants ($)

Moderate

Winter lends its own special majesty to Yosemite National Park

By any standards, Yosemite is the most spectacular national park in the country. To call it awe-inspiring would be an understatement.

Nearly 70 percent of the annual visitors to Yosemite National Park arrive in the summer and stay within the compact but awesome Yosemite Valley. The main section of the park, just 7sq miles (18sq km) in area, boasts monumental granite walls and high-diving waterfalls, but there remains almost 1,200sq miles (3,076sq km) of splendor to explore. Beyond are such natural wonders as giant sequoias, alpine meadows, lakes and trout-filled streams, Glacier Point and majestic 13,000-ft (3,963-m) Sierra Nevada peaks. Giant sequoias are located in the Mariposa Grove, near the park's south entrance, about 30 miles (48km) from Yosemite Valley. In this great forest, over 200 trees measure more than 10ft (3m) in diameter.

Some of the park's finest scenery is in the wild back country along the Tioga Road. There are rustic lodges and campgrounds (permit camping). In the main valley, 3,500-ft (1,067-m) El Capitan attracts climbers from around the world.

Off-season visits are also spectacular. In fall, leaves turn from green to crimson and gold and nights are cool and pleasant. Spring offers magnificent waterfalls that create rainbows across the valley floor. For the ambitious, there's the 200-mile (322-km) John Muir Trail that follows the naturalist's path through the wilderness. For many, the winter provides solitude and restores the raw grandeur of the park. The ski season at Badger Pass lasts from the end of November until mid-April.

What To See

Above: *Cable-car, San Francisco—a fun way to travel around the city*

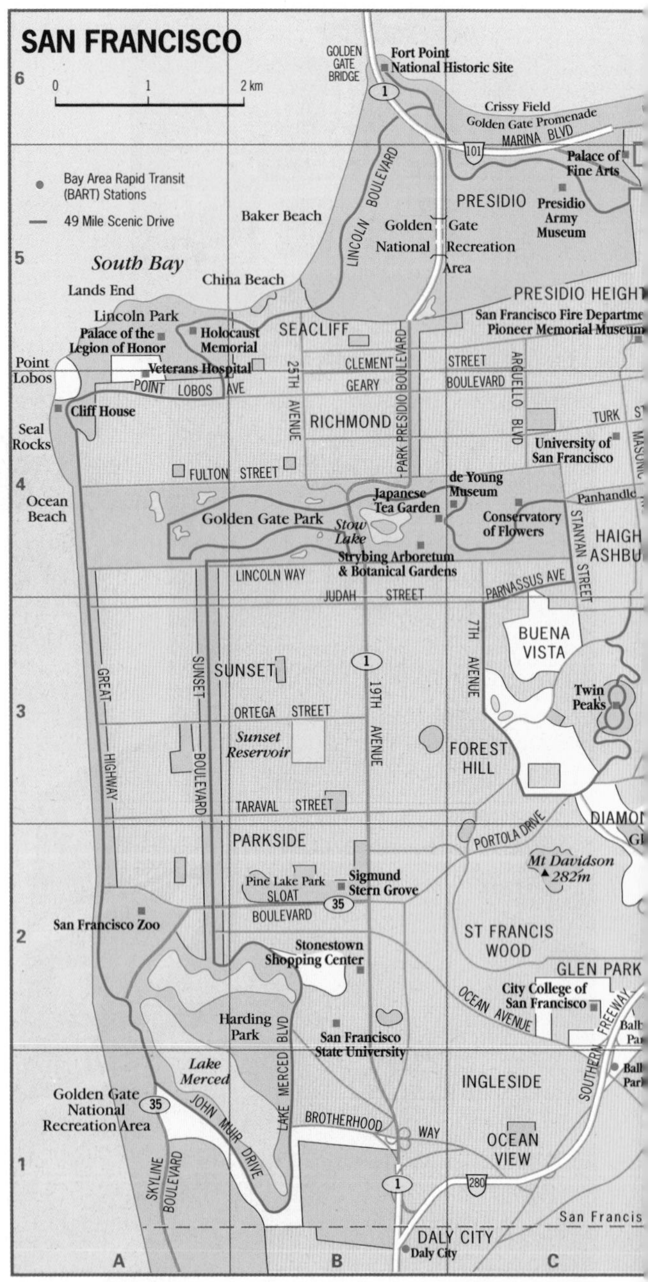
SAN FRANCISCO
0
1
2 km
Bay Area Rapid Transit (BART) Stations
49 Mile Scenic Drive
GOLDEN GATE BRIDGE
Fort Point National Historic Site
Crissy Field
Golden Gate Promenade
MARINA BLVD
Palace of Fine Arts
PRESIDIO
Presidio Army Museum
Baker Beach
LINCOLN BOULEVARD
Golden Gate National Recreation Area
South Bay
Lands End
China Beach
PRESIDIO HEIGHT
San Francisco Fire Departme Pioneer Memorial Museum
Lincoln Park
Palace of the Legion of Honor
Holocaust Memorial
SEACLIFF
Point Lobos
Veterans Hospital
CLEMENT STREET
GEARY BOULEVARD
ARGUELLO BLVD
POINT LOBOS AVE
25TH AVENUE
PARK PRESIDIO BOULEVARD
Cliff House
RICHMOND
TURK
Seal Rocks
University of San Francisco
FULTON STREET
de Young Museum
Ocean Beach
Japanese Tea Garden
Panhandle
Golden Gate Park
Stow Lake
Conservatory of Flowers
STANYAN STREET
HAIGH ASHBU
Strybing Arboretum & Botanical Gardens
LINCOLN WAY
PARNASSUS AVE
JUDAH STREET
BUENA VISTA
7TH AVENUE
SUNSET
GREAT HIGHWAY
SUNSET BOULEVARD
19TH AVENUE
Twin Peaks
ORTEGA STREET
Sunset Reservoir
FOREST HILL
TARAVAL STREET
DIAMO
PARKSIDE
PORTOLA DRIVE
Mt Davidson 282m
Pine Lake Park
Sigmund Stern Grove
SLOAT BOULEVARD
San Francisco Zoo
ST FRANCIS WOOD
Stonestown Shopping Center
GLEN PARK
City College of San Francisco
OCEAN AVENUE
SOUTHERN FREEWAY
Harding Park
San Francisco State University
Lake Merced
LAKE MERCED BLVD
INGLESIDE
Golden Gate National Recreation Area
JOHN MUIR DRIVE
BROTHERHOOD WAY
OCEAN VIEW
SKYLINE BOULEVARD
San Francis
DALY CITY
Daly City
A
B
C
1
2
3
4
5
6
1
35
101
280

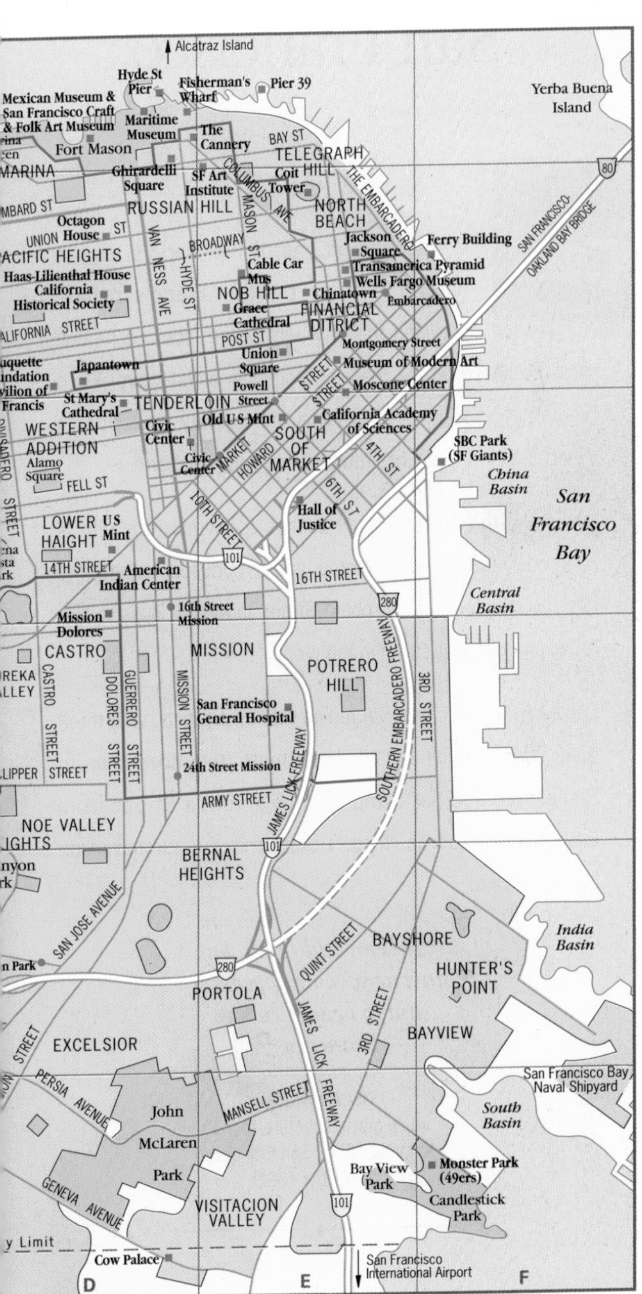

Alcatraz Island
Hyde St Pier
Fisherman's Wharf
Pier 39
Yerba Buena Island
Mexican Museum & San Francisco Craft & Folk Art Museum
Maritime Museum
The Cannery
Fort Mason
BAY ST
TELEGRAPH HILL
MARINA
Ghirardelli Square
SF Art Institute
Coit Tower
COLUMBUS AVE
THE EMBARCADERO
80
RUSSIAN HILL
MASON ST
NORTH BEACH
Octagon House
UNION ST
BROADWAY
Jackson Square
Ferry Building
SAN FRANCISCO-OAKLAND BAY BRIDGE
PACIFIC HEIGHTS
VAN NESS AVE
HYDE ST
Cable Car Mus
Transamerica Pyramid
Wells Fargo Museum
Haas-Lilienthal House
California Historical Society
NOB HILL
Chinatown
Embarcadero
Grace Cathedral
FINANCIAL DISTRICT
CALIFORNIA STREET
POST ST
Montgomery Street
Union Square
Museum of Modern Art
Japantown
Powell Street
Moscone Center
St Mary's Cathedral
TENDERLOIN
Old US Mint
California Academy of Sciences
WESTERN ADDITION
Civic Center
SOUTH OF MARKET
SBC Park (SF Giants)
Alamo Square
FELL ST
MARKET
HOWARD
4TH ST
China Basin
10TH STREET
6TH ST
San Francisco Bay
LOWER HAIGHT
US Mint
Hall of Justice
101
14TH STREET
American Indian Center
16TH STREET
Central Basin
16th Street Mission
280
Mission Dolores
CASTRO
MISSION
POTRERO HILL
CASTRO STREET
DOLORES STREET
GUERRERO STREET
MISSION STREET
San Francisco General Hospital
SOUTHERN EMBARCADERO FREEWAY
3RD STREET
24th Street Mission
JAMES LICK FREEWAY
ARMY STREET
NOE VALLEY
BERNAL HEIGHTS
SAN JOSE AVENUE
India Basin
BAYSHORE
QUINT STREET
HUNTER'S POINT
PORTOLA
BAYVIEW
EXCELSIOR
PERSIA AVENUE
MANSELL STREET
San Francisco Bay Naval Shipyard
John McLaren Park
South Basin
Bay View Park
Monster Park (49ers)
Candlestick Park
GENEVA AVENUE
VISITACION VALLEY
Cow Palace
San Francisco International Airport
D
E
F

San Francisco

Its location on one of the world's largest natural harbors, the San Francisco Bay, provides this city with some fabulous natural views to backdrop the prevalent Victorian architecture. From hippie-haven Haight-Ashbury to the touristy Fisherman's Wharf, San Francisco has retained its historical charm.

Ironically, the horrible earthquakes for which this city is infamously known have created its most unusual feature: the hilly, twisting streets. Lombard Street, in swank Russian Hill, is "the crookedest street in the world."

Cable-cars make city travel fun as well as practical, with three main lines: Powell and Market streets from downtown to Fisherman's Wharf, and along California Street from Embarcadero to Van Ness. Tickets may be purchased on board the cars.

"It is an odd thing, but anyone who disappears is said to be seen in San Francisco."

OSCAR WILDE
while giving a lecture to the Bohemian Club, San Francisco (December 1882)

San Francisco

The Gold Rush of the mid-19th century brought a diverse ethnicity to San Francisco. Areas like Chinatown and North Beach have preserved their different native cultures.

Out in the bay to the north is the infamous Alcatraz Island, the site of the notorious former prison. It is easily seen from Coit Tower, on top of Telegraph Hill. Russian Hill provides a panoramic look at the Golden Gate Bridge and the bay. To the north and east of the city lie the Napa Valley and Marin County, where wine-tasting is the hobby of choice.

Few places in the world can boast the sophistication of a major metropolitan area while also being offset by 42 hills and, and at the same time, surrounded by the serenity of lush vineyards as does San Francisco.

Famously crooked Lombard Street

What to See in San Francisco

ALCATRAZ ✪✪✪

Of the 14 islands punctuating the massive San Francisco Bay, 12-acre (5-ha) Alcatraz is the most famous. Rising 135ft (41m) out of the bay, it is easy to see why it is nicknamed "The Rock." Although wild flowers are abundant on the island and the views of the bay and the Golden Gate bridge are breathtaking, most visitors visit the island to tour the massive fortress that covers most of the grounds. Built in 1858 as a military post, it soon became a military prison and finally a federal penitentiary.

Alcatraz can be reached by a short ferry crossing from Fisherman's Wharf

Because of the severe tides and undertow of the surrounding chilly waters, escape from the prison was reputed to be impossible. Three inmates dug their way out of their prison cells and disappeared in 1962. No one knows if they made it to the mainland, but their bodies were never found. The prison closed soon after the attempt, and a group of Native Americans claimed the island as their birthright. Some of the buildings were burned before the National Park Service took control and reopened Alcatraz as a tourist attraction in 1973.

Three prominent movies have been filmed on the island: *Escape from Alcatras, The Birdman of Alcatraz* and *The Rock.* Tours include a close-up look at the cells with audio-cassette narration by former prisoners and guards and exterior trail walks led by park rangers. Dress warmly and wear comfortable shoes.

- 29D6
- 415/705 5555
- Hours vary, advance reservations recommended
- Ferry from Pier 41, Fisherman's Wharf
- Moderate

Stone exhibit in the Asian Art Museum

ASIAN ART MUSEUM ✪✪

More than 40 Asian countries are represented in this museum, the largest of its kind outside the Asian continent. Exclusive to this museum are works of Asian art spanning 4,000 years of Chinese history. It also houses outstanding exhibits from India, Japan and Korea and more than 300 works from the estates of Chinese emperors. The msueum moved from its Golden Gate Park location to a grand, renovated space in the Civic Center in 2003.

www.asianart.org
- 29D4
- 200 Larkin Street, Civic Center
- 415/581 3500
- Tue–Sun 10–5, Thu 10–9
- Moderate, free 1st Tue of month

CABLE CAR MUSEUM AND POWERHOUSE VIEWING GALLERY ✪✪

If you're fascinated by San Francisco's cable-cars, visit this working nerve center and museum. On exhibit are the first cable-cars, which went unchanged for almost 100 years. Their design was modernized in 1982. Also housed in the three-level, red-brick 1907 barn are photographs, artifacts and a model collection. From the viewing gallery you can watch craftsmen working on the cars.

- 29E5
- 1201 Mason Street
- 415/474 1887
- Daily 10–5 (extended hours in spring and summer)
- Free

CALIFORNIA ACADEMY OF SCIENCES ✪✪✪

Dating back to the mid-19th century, this is considered one of the finest natural history museums in the world. It houses several galleries, an exhibit that allows visitors to "experience" an earthquake, and a hands-on Discovery Room for children. The Steinhart Aquarium has almost 14,000 salt-water species which include octopuses, sea-horses, dolphins and sharks. The ANTS exhibit showcases the nest building and food collecting behavior of six live ant colonies. The Howard Street location also has a nurturing place called the Nature Nest for young visitors. Note: The Academy has moved to temporary premises in Howard Street and is expected to return to Golden Gate Park in 2008.

- 29E4
- 875 Howard Street, between 4th and 5th streets
- 415/750 7145
- Daily 10–5 (extended hours in summer)
- Moderate; senior/children rates. Free 1st Wed of month

CALIFORNIA PALACE OF THE LEGION OF HONOR ✪✪✪

Refurbished in 1995, this classical palace was inspired by the Hotel de Salm in Paris, the site where Napoleon established the Legion D'Honneur. The Palace houses an extraordinary collection of 75,000 prints and drawings from the Achenbach Foundation, and expansive European art dating from 2500BC through to the 20th century. Rodin's *The Thinker* is on display in the courtyard.

- 28A5
- 34th Avenue and Clement Street, Lincoln Park
- 415/750 3600
- Tue–Sun 9.30–5
- Moderate; senior/children rates; free every Tue

CARTOON ART MUSEUM ✪

This museum houses permanent and rotating exhibits of original two- and three-dimensional art and cartoon objects. You can see the original artwork and drawings used in the production of cartoons. Some exhibits go back to the 18th century. Video presentations are also part of the program.

www.cartoonart.org
- 29D3
- 655 Mission Street
- 415/227 8666
- Tue–Sun 11–5. Closed holidays
- Moderate; senior/children rates

CHINESE HISTORICAL SOCIETY OF AMERICA ✪✪✪

The largest collection of Chinese-American objects in the US is housed here, including Chinese dragon heads, an 1880 Buddhist altar and a concise history of the Chinese experience in America, from 1840 to the present day.

- 29D5
- 965 Clay Street
- 415/391 1188
- Tue–Fri noon–5, Sat–Sun noon–4
- Inexpensive

CIVIC CENTER PLAZA ✪✪

Dominated by the French Renaissance-inspired City Hall, the complex dates back to the 1906 earthquake. On the west end is the War Memorial and Performing Arts Center. The Center is home to the Louise M. Davies Symphony Hall, the War Memorial Opera House and the War Memorial Veterans Building. The latter contains the San Francisco Museum of Modern Art and the Herbst Theatre, where the United Nations charter was signed in 1945. Other classically styled buildings in the plaza complex are the Civic Auditorium, the San Francisco Public Library and the State Building.

- 29D4
- Van Ness Avenue/Polk Street at Grove and McAllister streets
- 415/554 4858 (information); 415/554 4933 (tour manager)
- Free

City Hall epitomizes the Beaux-Arts style

A Walk Around Chinatown

This walk takes you through the largest Chinese community outside Asia.

Enter through the Chinatown Gate, at Bush Street and Grant Avenue.

Note the dragon-entwined lampposts and pagoda roofs as you are greeted by a cacophony of Chinese street merchants and the aromas of simmering noodles.

Walk north on Grant to the Dragon House Antiques (No. 455).

Continue up Grant to St. Mary's Park where there's a 12-ft (3.5-m) sculpture of Sun Yat-sen.

Continue north to Clay, turn right to Kearny, then left to Portsmouth Square. Across Kearny is the Holiday Inn.

Pop inside to the Chinese Cultural Center.

Go north on Kearny, to Pacific, then left to the New Asia restaurant (No. 772).

This is a good choice for lunch.

Continue east on Pacific to Grant, then go left two blocks to Washington. Turn right.

Admire the three-tiered pagoda-style Bank of Canton, then continue west to the Tien Hou Temple (in Waverly Place on Washington). Around the corner is The Great China Herb Co. (No. 857), for herbal prescriptions.

Continue west on Washington to Stockton, then turn left.

The Chinese Six Companies building (No. 843) is an architectural wonder, with its curved roof tiles and elaborate cornices.

Walk south on Stockton to the Stockton Street Tunnel. A 15-minute walk through the tunnel brings you to downtown Union Square.

Distance
5 miles (8km)

Time
2–4 hours

Start point
Chinatown Gate

29E5

End point
Union Square
29E5

Lunch
New Asia ($$)
772 Pacific Avenue
415/391 6666

Chinatown lion

29D6
North of North Beach
Cafés, stands ($)
Excellent

FISHERMAN'S WHARF

Bustling Fisherman's Wharf is the center of San Francisco's thriving tourist trade. It has many shops, street stands, food emporia and the like. Originally, it was an active base for San Francisco Bay's once busy fishing industry, until the late 1940s. A small fleet still operates.

28B5
GGNRA, Building 201, Fort Mason, San Francisco, CA 94123
415/561 4700; 415/752 4227 (Japanese Tea Garden)
Cafés, stands ($)
Excellent
Moderate

GOLDEN GATE NATIONAL RECREATION AREA

This huge area takes in Golden Gate Park with its museums, open-air performances and sporting events (► 19). Once an expanse of sand dunes, the area has been transformed into a botanical masterpiece. The Strybing Arboretum and Botanical Gardens near the museum complex encompass 70 acres (28ha) of plant life. The Japanese Tea Garden, with koi ponds and an 18th-century Buddha, is one of the most interesting spots in all San Francisco. The children's playground has a working carousel, and the park is host to dozens of cultural fairs and exhibits, and also food- and wine-tastings. In summer, there are operas and a popular Shakespearean festival.

Near the Golden Gate Bridge, the historical Fort Mason Center, once an embarkation point for American soldiers, houses a youth hostel, several theaters, the African-American Historical and Cultural Society, the Museo Italo-Americano, the Mexican Museum (due to move location) and the SS *Jeremiah O'Brien*. A Golden Gate Explorer Pass provides unlimited admission to all museums and gardens for six months.

The Japanese Tea Garden at Golden Gate Park

Did you know ?

For thousands of years, the only inhabitants near the current Golden Gate region were the Native American Ohlones, a sub-tribe of the Coast Miwok. Feasting mainly on oysters, they left huge piles of the shells which can still be seen. The largest pile is located at Coyote Hills, in southern Alameda County.

GRACE CATHEDRAL

Taking over a half-century to build, this marvellous structure is a near-perfect replica of a Florentine cathedral. The singing of the Vespers each Thursday at 5.15pm is a truly spiritual experience.

29E5
1100 California Street
415/749 6300
Free, but donations accepted

HYDE STREET PIER AND HISTORICAL SHIPS

In the Fisherman's Wharf area, this pier is the permanent home of several historical ships. Here you will find the ferry boat *Eureka* (1890), once the world's largest ferry boat, and the *Balclutha*, a square-rigged sailing ship from Scotland (1886), famed for rounding Cape Horn several times. Before leaving the area, drop into the National Maritime Museum at nearby Aquatic Park.

29D6
415/561 7100
Daily 10–5
Inexpensive. National Park Golden Eagle Pass free

LOMBARD STREET 

Located in the Russian Hill district, this is San Francisco's famous "crookedest" street. Traffic zigzags down it at 5mph (8kph), moving around colorful gardens which were established in the 1920s.

29D5
Between Hyde and Leavenworth streets

MISSION SAN FRANCISCO DE ASIS (MISSION DOLORES) 

Founded in 1776 and moved to its present site in 1782, the mission is thought to be the oldest standing structure in the city. Adjoining is the Mission Dolores Basilica, the least changed of all California's existing missions. The architecture of Mission Dolores is a combination of Moorish, Mission and Corinthian styles, and the garden cemetery is filled with the burial sites of San Francisco pioneers.

29D4
16th and Dolores streets
415/621 8203
Daily 9–4.30 (until 4 in fall and winter)
Inexpensive

Stained glass at Mission Dolores, the sixth of 21 Missions founded by the Spanish in California

28C4
2501 Irving Street (at 26th Avenue)
415/750 3600
Tue–Sat 10–4.45
Free

DE YOUNG MUSEUM

Reopened in 2005 as the de Young Museum, the museum contains a collection of American artwork in a 22-gallery complex set in Golden Gate Park. The museum's exhibits include paintings, sculpture, decorative arts, textiles and furniture. Some of the artwork dates to the mid-17th century. Also on display are classical and tribal works.

68B3
West Cliff Drive
831/423 4609
Beach daily 8–dusk; visitor center 10–4
Inexpensive

NATURAL BRIDGES STATE BEACH

Set in 65 acres (26ha), this beach, just before Santa Cruz, is a wonderful place to observe the migration of the colorful Monarch butterfly between mid-October and February. There are also tide pools to explore, as well as ecological and wildlife exhibits in the visitor center.

29E5

Coit Tower
415/362 0808
Daily 10–6.30
Inexpensive (to go to top of tower)

NORTH BEACH

This thriving, trendy neighborhood, on the northeastern tip of San Francisco, is bound by Chinatown, the Financial District and Russian Hill. North Beach has a distinctly Italian atmosphere, and is central to most attractions, shops and restaurants in the area. Its heyday in the 1950s saw Jack Kerouac and other Beat Generation poets frequenting the cafés and bookstores, which remain important cultural meeting places. At the center of the neighborhood is **Coit Tower**, an impressive 210-ft (64-m) landmark, built in 1934, reached on foot via the Filbert Steps by Darnell Place.

The Palace of Fine Arts, designed as a Roman ruin, incorporates a classical domed rotunda as its centerpiece

28C5
3601 Lyon Street
415/561 0360
Tue–Sun 10–5; open on Mon hols
Moderate, free 1st Wed of month

PALACE OF FINE ARTS

This Bernard Maybeck Greco-Romanesque rotunda is one of the most photographed buildings in San Francisco. Levelled by the great earthquake of 1906, it was completely rebuilt in 1915 and today presents continuing cultural events. Inside the complex is the Exploratorium, a wonderful hands-on science museum, ideal for families, with toys disguised as science education.

ST. MARY'S CATHEDRAL OF THE ASSUMPTION ✪✪✪

The radical architecture by Pietro Belluschi and Pier Luigi Nervi caused great debate during construction. Rising on concrete pylons to a height of 190ft (58m), the exterior resembles a washing machine agitator. Inside, however, the soaring cruciform is nothing short of breathtaking. The majestic pipe organ, itself, is worth seeing.

- 29D4
- 1111 Gough Street
- 415/567 2020
- Mon–Fri 7–5, Sun 7–6.30
- Free, but donations accepted

SFMOMA: One of the finest museums of modern art in the country

SAN FRANCISCO MUSEUM OF MODERN ART ✪✪✪

Devoted solely to modern art and occupying a quarter-million sq ft, this is the main structure in the Yerba Buena Arts Center (SoMo district). Exhibits include a world-renowned collection of photography, and 20th-century works from such artists as Dali, O'Keefe and Jasper Johns. A current feature exhibit is "From Matisse to Diebenkorn: Works from the Permanent Collection."

- 29E5
- 151 Third Street
- 415/357 4000
- Mon, Tue, Fri–Sun 11–5.45; Thu 11–8.45
- Moderate, senior/student rates, free 1st Tue of month

SAUSALITO ✪

This is the first small town in Marin County after crossing the Golden Gate Bridge. Once a fishing town, it has unfortunately been overrun with tacky tourist shops and no longer has the great charm of years past.

- 68B4
- 5 miles (8km) north of San Francisco
- Ferry from Ferry Building or Fisherman's Wharf

TRANSAMERICA PYRAMID ✪✪

Depending on who you ask, this structure is either a landmark or an eyesore. Completed in 1972, the pyramid skyscraper juts 853ft (260m) skyward, making it the tallest building in San Francisco.

- 29E5
- 600 Montgomery Street
- Mon–Fri 8–4

Food & Drink

Because of its immensely diverse cultural make-up, California is a food lover's paradise. The major cities have authentic cuisine from almost every nation in the world.

Cuisine

Nearby Mexico exerts a strong influence, especially encouraging the generous use of avocados and salsa. There are tacquerias everywhere. Cilantro is the spice of choice.

Sushi is fresh and popular. Chinese food, especially in San Francisco's Chinatown, is excellent. Fine dining establishments in the major cities feature delicious French cuisine.

All along the Coast are seafood houses to fit every budget. Fresh tuna and black cod are popular, while crab, oysters and jumbo shrimp cocktails satisfy lighter appetites.

North Beach in San Francisco has the best

Below: *Crab vendor on Fisherman's Wharf*
Right: *Delicious seafood dishes are on offer all along the coast*

authentic Italian food, pasta can be found everywhere, Beverly Hills has great Jewish delis and Solvang (Central Coast) features fine Scandinavian food.

Most visitors to the area, however, look forward to sampling genuine California cuisine. Menus are renowned for catering to swimsuit figures by being light, healthy and diet-friendly. For vegetarians, there is a huge year-round variety of locally grown vegetables (steamed), fresh salads with gourmet greens, and fresh fruits. Non-meat burgers and chicken are popular. The finest steaks can also be found, especially around the northern farming areas.

Lori's Diner—a popular venue

For a busy day of sightseeing, there are literally thousands of fast-food establishments. Even most of the small, inland towns have the major chains. In-N-Out Burger is a good choice for those on the run.

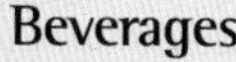

Beverages

Health-conscious Californians consume more bottled water per capita than any other state in the US. This may be due to the fact that a large part of the state has a desert-like climate and bottled water is easy to carry. Restaurants and markets offer a wide selection of both carbonated and uncarbonated types. Especially in the Palm Springs area, there are many roadside stands offering tasty "date shakes."

Although there are a few local breweries, imported beers seem to be favored by the locals, so you can find almost any of the popular brands. Mexico's Corona is a top choice. Micro-breweries are also popular, so check out some of the local beer-bistros for thirst-quenching treats.

The Mexican margarita is a time-tested standard. The martini is said to have originated in San Francisco and the Mai Tai cocktail was invented at Trader Vic's, at the original location in Oarkland.

Wine is said to appease and to have dietary and health considerations. Because so much excellent wine is produced in the state, the selection is overwhelming and costs are relatively affordable. Wineries of great renown include Mondavi, Beringer, Domaine Chandon, Louis M. Martini, Buena Vista, Sebastiani and Korbel Champagne. A favorite is Mondavi's unfiltered Cabernet Sauvigon, while Pinot Noirs and Syrahs are also becoming increasingly popular. Along with the world-famous Napa Valley and Sonoma wines, the wineries of the central coastal area are gaining in prominence.

Star Gazing

When dining and drinking in LA, remember that "star-gazing" may not necessarily be an exercise in astronomy. You could find yourself rubbing elbows with a celebrity straight off the screen as you satisfy your appetite. There is year-round patio dining, and casual attire is the norm. Most establishments accept all major credit cards.

Californian wines are in a class of their own

29D5

Octagon House
2645 Gough Street
415/441 7512
2nd and 4th Thu and 2nd Sun of each month (except Jan), noon–3. Closed holidays
Contributions

UNION STREET ✪✪✪

Union Street runs east–west from Montgomery Street in North Beach to the Presidio. It is one of the city's most fashionable areas in which to live and shop, and with its many beautifully restored Victorian mansions that have been converted into boutiques, art galleries and cafés, it is a must-see. Scattered among the bustling retail spots are several landmarks that should not be missed. The **Octagon House** (just off Union Street) is a pale-blue, eight-sided structure that features antique furniture from the 18th and 19th centuries. Also of interest is an exhibit containing the signatures of 54 of the 56 original signatories of the Declaration of Independence.

68B3
Bay and High Street
831/459 4008
Student-led tours Mon–Fri 10.30, 1.30
Free, parking inexpensive

UNIVERSITY OF CALIFORNIA AT SANTA CRUZ ✪

On the campus are the remains of several buildings from the Cowell Ranch, dating back to the mid-19th century. Other outstanding buildings include two art galleries and the Long Marine Aquarium. The most popular exhibit in the aquarium is a virtually flawless skeleton of a blue whale. Eight colleges make up this 2,000-acre (810-ha) site, overlooking Monterey Bay and Santa Cruz.

29E5
420 Montgomery Street
415/396 2619
Mon–Fri 9–5. Closed bank holidays
Free

WELLS FARGO HISTORY MUSEUM 

Located in the Wells Fargo Bank Building, the museum contains artifacts from the Old West and the California Gold Rush, and records the rise and fall of the company. There is a superbly preserved stagecoach and other interesting pieces from early years to the present.

A Drive Through Marin County

This drive takes you through scenic Marin County.

Begin at the Presidio in north San Francisco. Cross the Golden Gate Bridge and continue north on Highway 101.

Sausalito (➤ 39) is to your left.

A dramatic panorama unfolds from the summit of Mount Tamalpais

Proceed north to the Tamalpais Valley exit and follow the signs to Muir Woods National Monument.

Here you can enjoy the beauty of the redwoods.

Return to the 101 and continue northward.

Stop at the Marin County Civic Center, an architectural masterpiece designed by Frank Lloyd Wright in 1957.

Backtrack along the 101, through San Rafael, to Highway 580. Follow it across the Richmond-San Rafael Bridge.

Right before the bridge is San Quentin Prison. As you cross the bridge, San Francisco Bay is on your right and San Pablo Bay on your left.

A short distance past the bridge, take the 80 Freeway south to Berkeley.

Sites to see on the University of Berkeley campus include the Botanical Garden, Lawrence Hall of Science and the Phoebe Apperson Hearst Museum of Anthropology.

Continuing back on the 80 southbound, follow the highway past Emeryville and across the San Francisco-Oakland Bay Bridge.

Look right to see Treasure Island Naval Station and Alcatraz (➤ 32).

Take the first exit off the bridge to Fisherman's Wharf.

Distance
120 miles (194km)

Time
6–8 hours, depending on time spent at attractions

Start point
The Presidio
28C5

End point
Fisherman's Wharf
29D6

Lunch
Dipsea Cafe ($$)
200 Shoreline Highway/Highway 1, Mill Valley
415/381 0298
Daily 7am–3pm
also at
2200 Fourth Street, San Rafael
415/459 0700
Daily 7am–3pm

Los Angeles

Whether you come for the beaches, mountains, museums or movie stars, Los Angeles teems with activity. Bring your sunglasses and your tanning lotion because here in California there is plenty of sunshine. For dedicated sun-seekers, beautiful beaches stretch along the western edge of this seemingly endless metropolis. Zuma Beach is one of the best for enjoying the pastime made famous by the music of The Beach Boys—surfing.

At Venice Beach you can either stroll barefoot along the beach or join the hustle along the Boardwalk, where vendors hawk their souvenirs. This is home to some of the nation's most colorful characters: musicians, magicians and mime artists, as well as Muscle Beach body builders.

"Call Los Angeles any dirty name you like—Six Suburbs in Search of a City, Paradise with a Lobotomy, anything—but the fact remains that you are already living in it before you get there."

AUSTRALIAN CRITIC
CLIVE JAMES,
London Observer (1979)

A distinctive LA landmark, the folk art extravaganza of Watts Towers

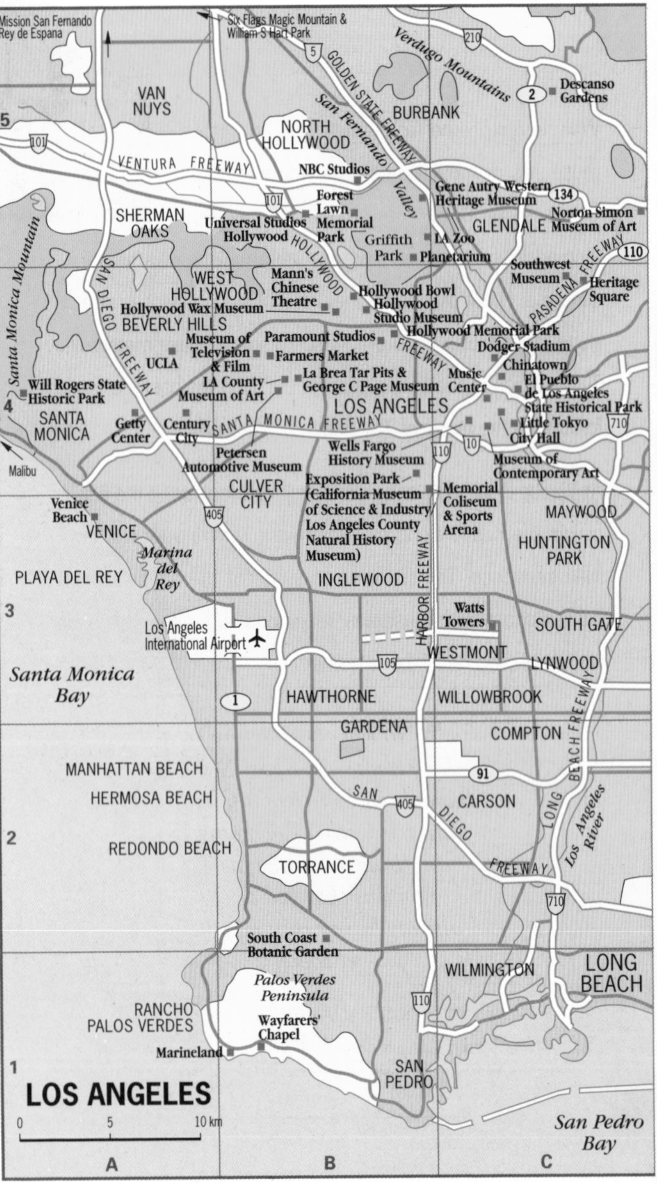

Mission San Fernando Rey de Espana
Six Flags Magic Mountain & William S Hart Park
Verdugo Mountains
Descanso Gardens
VAN NUYS
BURBANK
NORTH HOLLYWOOD
GOLDEN STATE FREEWAY
San Fernando Valley
VENTURA FREEWAY
NBC Studios
Gene Autry Western Heritage Museum
Forest Lawn Memorial Park
SHERMAN OAKS
Universal Studios Hollywood
Norton Simon Museum of Art
GLENDALE
Griffith Park
LA Zoo
Planetarium
Santa Monica Mountain
HOLLYWOOD
PASADENA FREEWAY
Southwest Museum
Heritage Square
Mann's Chinese Theatre
WEST HOLLYWOOD
Hollywood Bowl
Hollywood Wax Museum
Hollywood Studio Museum
SAN DIEGO FREEWAY
BEVERLY HILLS
Hollywood Memorial Park
Paramount Studios
Museum of Television & Film
Farmers Market
Dodger Stadium
UCLA
FREEWAY
Chinatown
LA County Museum of Art
La Brea Tar Pits & George C Page Museum
Music Center
El Pueblo de Los Angeles State Historical Park
Will Rogers State Historic Park
LOS ANGELES
SANTA MONICA
Getty Center
Century City
SANTA MONICA FREEWAY
Little Tokyo
City Hall
Malibu
Petersen Automotive Museum
Wells Fargo History Museum
Museum of Contemporary Art
CULVER CITY
Exposition Park (California Museum of Science & Industry, Los Angeles County Natural History Museum)
Memorial Coliseum & Sports Arena
Venice Beach
VENICE
MAYWOOD
HUNTINGTON PARK
Marina del Rey
PLAYA DEL REY
INGLEWOOD
HARBOR FREEWAY
Watts Towers
SOUTH GATE
Los Angeles International Airport
WESTMONT
LYNWOOD
Santa Monica Bay
HAWTHORNE
WILLOWBROOK
GARDENA
COMPTON
LONG BEACH FREEWAY
MANHATTAN BEACH
HERMOSA BEACH
SAN DIEGO FREEWAY
CARSON
Los Angeles River
REDONDO BEACH
TORRANCE
South Coast Botanic Garden
WILMINGTON
LONG BEACH
Palos Verdes Peninsula
RANCHO PALOS VERDES
Wayfarers' Chapel
Marineland
SAN PEDRO
San Pedro Bay
5 4 3 2 1
A B C
101 5 210 2 134 110 10 710 405 105 1 91

LOS ANGELES

0 5 10 km

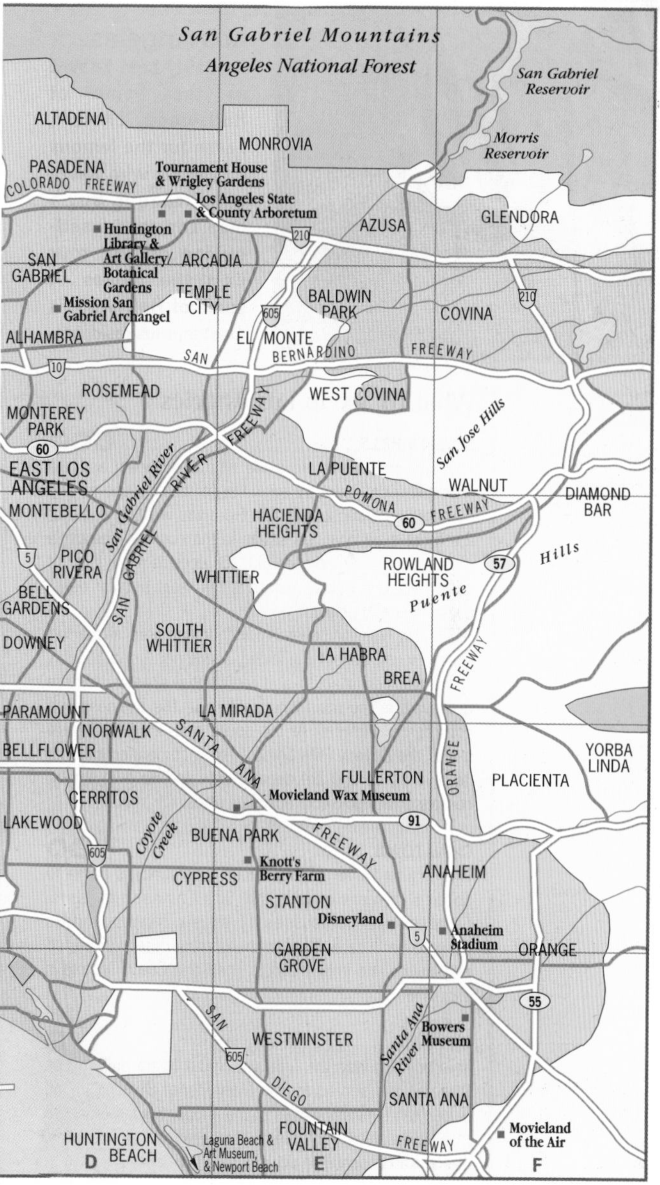

San Gabriel Mountains
Angeles National Forest
San Gabriel Reservoir
ALTADENA
MONROVIA
Morris Reservoir
PASADENA
Tournament House & Wrigley Gardens
COLORADO FREEWAY
Los Angeles State & County Arboretum
Huntington Library & Art Gallery/ Botanical Gardens
210
AZUSA
GLENDORA
SAN GABRIEL
ARCADIA
TEMPLE CITY
Mission San Gabriel Archangel
BALDWIN PARK
210
COVINA
605
ALHAMBRA
EL MONTE
SAN BERNARDINO FREEWAY
10
ROSEMEAD
WEST COVINA
MONTEREY PARK
San Jose Hills
60
EAST LOS ANGELES
LA PUENTE
WALNUT
POMONA FREEWAY
DIAMOND BAR
MONTEBELLO
San Gabriel River
SAN GABRIEL RIVER FREEWAY
HACIENDA HEIGHTS
60
5
PICO RIVERA
ROWLAND HEIGHTS
57
Puente Hills
BELL GARDENS
WHITTIER
DOWNEY
SOUTH WHITTIER
LA HABRA
BREA
FREEWAY
PARAMOUNT
LA MIRADA
NORWALK
SANTA ANA FREEWAY
BELLFLOWER
YORBA LINDA
ORANGE
FULLERTON
PLACIENTA
CERRITOS
Movieland Wax Museum
LAKEWOOD
91
Coyote Creek
BUENA PARK
605
Knott's Berry Farm
CYPRESS
ANAHEIM
STANTON
Disneyland
5
Anaheim Stadium
GARDEN GROVE
ORANGE
55
Santa Ana River
Bowers Museum
SAN DIEGO FREEWAY
WESTMINSTER
605
SANTA ANA
HUNTINGTON BEACH
Laguna Beach & Art Museum, & Newport Beach
FOUNTAIN VALLEY
Movieland of the Air
D
E
F

One of Hollywood's landmark hotels

Los Angeles

Probably best known as the home of Hollywood, LA is a haven for the famous and those who never quite made it. Buy a map and take a self-guided driving tour past the homes of some of Hollywood's most famous residents.

What to See in Los Angeles

46A4
Visitors Bureau, 239 S Beverly Drive, Beverly Hills 90212
310/248 1015

BEVERLY HILLS ✪✪✪

The City of Stars is the place where shopping and the entertainment industry each vie for their place as the number one attraction (➤ 49). Here you will find some of the most expensive real estate in the country. The city's most recognizable zip code (90210) receives more than 14 million visitors a year, making it the most popular destination in Los Angeles.

Beverly Hills has several main thoroughfares, all running east to west. Sunset Boulevard, at the north end, roughly splits the commercial and residential areas. Wilshire Boulevard is the main thoroughfare to the business and commercial centers. At the south end, Pico Boulevard marks the Beverly Hills border. This incorporated city has its own police and fire departments and its own library, complete with gold-colored library cards.

46C4
900 block of Broadway

CHINATOWN ✪✪

The cultural center of this unique community is home to about 5 percent of LA's 200,000 Chinese residents. Chinatown encompasses 16 square blocks, and its downtown area is filled with Asian architecture, good restaurants and import shops. The Kong Chow Temple is exquisite.

46C4
200 N Spring Street
213/978 0721
Mon–Fri 9–4
Free

CITY HALL 

This building was the first skyscraper to be built in Los Angeles and served as The Daily Planet Building in the *Superman* television series of the 1950s. Guided tours are free—weekdays from 10am–1pm—and last 45 minutes. There is an observation deck on the 27th floor.

A Walk Around Beverly Hills

This walk begins on one of the most expensive shopping streets in the world.

Walk north from Wilshire on Rodeo Drive.

Do a spot of window-shopping in Tiffany's, Saks and other high end boutiques (► 107).

Proceed north several blocks to Little Santa Monica, then go east (right) a couple of blocks to Crescent.

On the corner of Crescent you'll see the historic former Beverly Hills Post Office and the magnificent Beverly Hills Municipal Building. The latter houses City Hall and the Beverly Hills library and police station.

Take a left on Crescent and proceed north across Santa Monica Boulevard and through the Beverly Hills "flatlands."

The homes along here are absolutely gorgeous.

At Sunset Boulevard, walk across to the newly restored Beverly Hills Hotel (► 101).

Take a few minutes to stroll through the splendid lobby.

Proceed east on Sunset to the West Hollywood business district.

Here you will pass the famous Roxy theater, Spago restaurant and The Whiskey A Go-Go.

Continue east, stopping for lunch at the chic Sunset Plaza, then on to Sunset. Turn right on Crescent Heights Road and go south to Melrose Avenue. Turn left on to Melrose and walk several blocks to Fairfax Avenue.

At this corner is the sprawling CBS Television City. Tours are available, as well as free tickets to live tapings of television shows.

South of CBS is the Farmers' Market and the Grove, where your tour ends.

Distance
4 miles (6.5km)

Time
3–4 hours, depending on time spent at attractions

Start point
Beverly Hills, corner of Wilshire and Rodeo
46A4

End point
Farmers' Market and the Grove complex of shops, restaurants and movie theaters
46A4

Lunch
Chin Chin ($)
8618 Sunset Boulevard
310/652 1818

Farmers' Market is a mix of fruit and vegetable stalls, souvenir shops and food stands

A street market in El Pueblo State Historic Park

DESCANSO GARDENS ✪✪

46C5
1418 Descanso Drive, La Cañada Flintridge
818/949 4200
Daily 9–4.30. Closed Christmas Day
Moderate, special discounts

These glorious gardens cover 65 acres (26ha), including a 30-acre (12-ha) California live oak forest. Over 100,000 camellias collected from around the world florish here, as do many roses, lilacs and other blossoms. The Japanese Garden has a serene teahouse. It is worth the short drive north of the city.

EL PUEBLO DE LOS ANGELES STATE HISTORICAL PARK

46C4
Betweeen Alameda, Arcadia, Spring and Macy streets
213/628 1274
Hours vary call for information
Free

Here, on 44 acres (18ha) near downtown, you can visit the Avila Adobe (the oldest adobe house), Masonic Hall, Old Plaza Church and Sepulveda House. Founded in 1781, the main attraction for most visitors is Olvera Street, an open-air Mexican-style market place lined with specialty shops, vendors, cafés and restaurants.

EXPOSITION PARK ✪✪✪

46B4

California Museum of Science and Industry
Exposition Boulevard at Figueroa
213/744 7400
Daily 10–5
Free, charge for IMAX

California Afro-American Museum
213/744 7432
Wed–Sat 10–4
Free ($6 parking fee)

LA County Museum of Natural History
213/763 3466
Mon–Fri 9.30–5, Sat, Sun 10–5
Moderate, free first Tue of month

The Los Angeles Memorial Coliseum was host to the Olympics in 1932 and 1984. Several museums are contained within, including the **California Museum of Science and Industry**, with interactive exhibits, Aerospace Complex and the surround-vision IMAX theater, featuring a five-story-high screen. Other museums include the **California Afro-American** and the **Los Angeles County Museum of Natural History**, with three floors of dinosaur, fossil and cultural exhibits.

Did you know ?

Comedian Robin Williams said of Hollywood, "Living in Hollywood is like being in high school—only with money."

FOREST LAWN MEMORIAL PARK ✪✪

A cemetery may seem like an unusual attraction, but there are 300 lush acres (121ha) of grounds here, with reproductions of such works as da Vinci's *Last Supper*, and the world's largest religious painting on canvas, Jan Styke's *The Crucifixion*. Also not to be missed are the ornate tombstones of celebrities and the beautiful gardens. Forest Lawn cemetery is the final resting place of such Hollywood film legends as Humphrey Bogart, Errol Flynn, Spencer Tracy, Stan Laurel, Carole Lombard, W. C. Fields, Jean Harlow and Cary Grant.

46B5
1712 South Glendale Avenue, Glendale
818/241 4151
Daily 8–5
Free

Statue in Forest Lawn Memorial Park

THE GETTY CENTER ✪✪✪

Opened in December 1997, this billion-dollar arts complex sits high on a hill off the 405 San Diego freeway to the north of the city. Although still in its infancy it seems destined to become one of LA's main attractions. With everything from Greek sculptures to paintings by European masters and modern photography, the museum is surrounded by ponds, beautiful landscaping and a fine herb garden.

46A4
Getty Center
1200 Getty Center Drive
310/440 7300
Tue–Thu, Sun 10–6, Fri, Sat 10–9
Free ($7 fee for parking)

GRIFFITH PARK ✪✪✪

Here, in the Santa Monica Mountain range, Griffith Park contains the LA Zoo, Griffith Observatory and Planetarium (closed for renovation until 2006), as well as Travel Town, an outdoor transportation museum. The Observatory is the perfect spot to view the Hollywood sign and the entire city, while the Planetarium features incredible laserium shows. There are horseback riding and children's rides and attractions, plus plenty of picnic areas.

46B5
Mount Hollywood
323/664 1191 (Observatory/Planetarium); 323/666 4650 (Zoo); 323/913 4688 (tourist information)
Hours vary so call for information.
The park is free; some attractions have moderate fees

HOLLYWOOD (➤ 21, TOP TEN)

HOLLYWOOD WAX MUSEUM ✪✪

Over 220 of Hollywood's greatest stars, political leaders and sports greats—all made of wax, but very lifelike—are on show at the Hollywood Wax Museum. Also included are displays on television, motion pictures and religion. Exhibits rotate every six months or so. The Chamber of Horrors is a favorite, as well as the recent additions of current stars.

46B4
6767 Hollywood Boulevard
323/462 8860
Sun–Thu 10–midnight, Fri–Sat to 1am
Moderate

HUNTINGTON LIBRARY, ART GALLERY AND BOTANICAL GARDENS

47D5
1151 Oxford Road, San Marino
626/405 2141
Tue–Fri 12–4.30pm, Sat–Sun 10.30–4.30
Moderate

The historical library contains over four million items, including art treasures and an extraordinary treasury of rare and precious manuscripts. After taking in the Huntington's art and books, take a walk through the immaculate botanical gardens, the best in the state. Here, 15 separate garden areas contain around 14,000 different types of plants and trees. Arrive early because the grounds fill up fast.

LITTLE TOKYO

46C4
First Street & Central Avenue

The city's Japanese quarter features the 40-shop Japanese Village Plaza, which resembles a rural village. Also here are Noguchi Plaza, with its fan-shaped Japan America Theatre, the Japanese American National Museum, and quiet Japanese gardens. Some great sushi bars can also be found here.

LONG BEACH

46C1
Pier J, Long Beach Harbor
562/435 3511
Daily 10–5
Free; moderate-priced guided tours

This rapidly growing city, just south of Los Angeles, is now California's fifth largest city. Its Shoreline Village and Wilmore Park surround the Convention and Entertainment Center, a popular corporate convention spot. Boats to Catalina Island depart from Golden Shore Boulevard.

Of special interest is the *Queen Mary*, which came to rest in Long Beach in 1967. With 12 decks and weighing in at 50,000 tons, it is the largest passenger ship ever built, the *crème de la crème* of 1932 art deco luxury. There are lots of shops and eateries on board.

LOS ANGELES STATE AND COUNTY ARBORETUM

47D5
301 N Baldwin Avenue, Arcadia
626/821 3222
Daily 9–4.30 (extended hours in summer)
Inexpensive; various discounts

The trees and shrubs in the 127-acre (51-ha) splendor of the Los Angeles Arboretum are arranged according to the

The delightful Queen Anne guest house in Los Angeles Arboretum

The cutting edge of contemporary sculpture on display at MOCA

continent they originate from. Also featured are greenhouses, a bird sanctuary and historic buildings like the Queen Anne Cottage, home of the estate's former owner, Elia Jackson Baldwin. Picnic areas and tours available.

MANN'S CHINESE THEATRE ✪✪✪

Originally Grauman's Chinese Theatre, Mann's, a prime Hollywood tourist attraction, is a good starting point for a tour of Los Angeles (➤ 21). The theater was opened in 1927 by showman Sid Grauman, and whenever a film was premiered here, stars left their hand or foot prints.

- 46B4
- 6925 Hollywood Boulevard
- 323/464 8111

MUSEUM OF CONTEMPORARY ART (MOCA) ✪✪✪

This seven-tiered museum (much of which is below street level) has 11 giant pyramidal skylights and a 53-ft (16-m) barrel-vaulted entrance. It is dedicated to works of art since the 1940s and features traveling exhibitions. Also at Geffen Contemporary and Pacific Design Center.

- 46B4
- 250 S Grand Avenue
- 213/621 2766
- Mon, Fri 11–5, Thu 11–8, Sat, Sun 11–6
- Moderate, free Thu

PETERSEN AUTOMOTIVE MUSEUM ✪✪✪

If you are an automotive fan, the Petersen Museum, with one of the largest auto collections in the world, is a must. It explores automotive history and culture from the earliest jalopies. Highlights are the 1957 Ferrari 250 Testa Rossa, and customized cars from Dean Jeffries and George Barris.

- 46B4
- 6060 Wilshire Boulevard
- 323/930 CARS
- Tue–Sun 10–6
- Moderate

SOUTHWEST MUSEUM ✪

This mission-revival style building, high above downtown LA, focuses on Native American art, including jewelry, basketwork and weaving. The museum's founder, Charles Lummis, director of the Los Angeles Library in 1907, also donated rare books to the museum.

- 46C4
- 234 Museum Drive
- 323/221 2164
- Tue–Sun 10–5
- Moderate

UNIVERSAL STUDIOS AND CITYWALK ✪✪✪

46B5
100 Universal City Plaza, Universal City
800-UNIVERSAL
Daily, from 9 or 10am; closing hours vary
Expensive

For a fascinating behind-the-scenes look at movie-making, plan to spend the better part of a day at Universal Studios, the world's biggest and busiest motion picture and television studio-cum-theme park. Citywalk features outdoor dining and a wide variety of shops that are a cut above what you might expect. There are huge outdoor screens that show music videos and movie previews and a theater complex shows all the latest movies.

The upper and lower sections are connected by a long escalator, making the 420-acre (170-ha) park easy to navigate. Some of the more interesting sets still standing are from such films as *The Sting, Animal House* and *Home Alone*. There are theme rides based on other successful films such as *Revenge of the Mummy* and *Jurassic Park*.

The beachfront, Venice Beach—haunt of skateboarders and rollerbladers

VENICE BEACH ✪✪

46A3
15 miles (24km) from downtown Los Angeles, access via Lincoln Boulevard

Just south along the beach from Santa Monica is Venice Beach. Although it appears to be a throwback to the 1960s, it is really a thriving enclave for modern bohemians. The neighborhood was founded in 1905 by Abbot Kinney, who hoped to create a haven for artistic types. Gondolas were imported from Italy and, for a time, the canals were eerily similar to those in Europe. Try a free self-guided tour. The most popular today is the Ocean Front Walk, teeming with visitors, street performers and souvenir stands. You can also rent a bicycle or rollerblades.

WATTS TOWERS ✪✪✪

46C3
1765 E 107th Street
213/847 4646

Italian immigrant Simon Rodia took 30 years to build these extraordinary towers by himself, using scraps of whatever materials he could find. Saved from demolition by local residents, the towers are currently being restored.

A Drive Around Los Angeles

This drive winds through some of LA's most exclusive neighborhoods, then west to Malibu.

From the Hollywood Bowl, drive north, veering to the left on to Cahuenga Boulevard. Drive to the Mulholland Drive turn-off, go left and continue on to Mulholland west.

Along Mulholland are several turn-offs for viewing the city and the San Fernando Valley below.

Continue westward on Mulholland to the 405 Freeway, entering southbound.

Take the first exit (Getty Center Drive), the site of the Getty Center (► 51).

Continue south on the 405 to Sunset Boulevard and exit. Turn right on to Sunset and drive westward. Continue to Bundy Drive and turn left at the light. Travel south about a mile (1.6km) to reach the stoplight at San Vincente. Go through the light, turn left and right to continue on Bundy.

Just past the next stop-light is the Simpson-Goldman murder scene, to your right.

Return to Sunset and turn left. Travel west on Sunset through the Pacific Palisades, to Pacific Coast Highway, along the ocean.

At the junction of Sunset and the Pacific Coast Highway is Gladstones 4 Fish, a great place to take lunch.

Continue north on Pacific Coast Highway to Malibu. Las Tunas State Beach is a good beach to spend time on. Continue north to Malibu Canyon Road and turn right at the light. Follow the road over the Santa Monica Mountains and turn into Las Virgines Road. Continue to the on-ramp to the 101 Freeway, and follow it south to the Highland exit and the Hollywood Bowl.

Distance
60 miles (97km)

Time
About 5 hours

Start/end point
Hollywood Bowl
46B4

Lunch
Gladstones 4 Fish ($$)
17300 Pacific Coast Highway, Pacific Palisades
310/454 3474

Hollywood landmark: Entrance to Paramount Studios

San Diego

The beautiful Mission Bay and world-famous San Diego Zoo are highlights of this city, one of the most laid-back areas in the US.

For excitement, there's Sea World or the San Diego Wild Animal Park. For serenity, the Japanese Friendship Garden's traditional sand-and-stone garden and wooded canyon view is the perfect picnic spot. Those interested in science will appreciate The Reuben H. Fleet Space Theater and Science Center. Its Space Theater's OMNIMAX films bring outer space up close, while the Aerospace Museum showcases heroes of aviation and space.

Old Town commemorates the first permanent settlement in California and still has many of the city's original buildings. Trolley tours through the six-block area make seeing the sights easy.

"Wouldn't it be wonderful to have a zoo in San Diego? I believe I'll build one."

DR. HENRY WEGEFORTH,
on hearing the roar of caged lions at
the California Panama
Exposition (1906)

The modern San Diego skyline

The lighthouse at Cabrillo National Monument

San Diego

San Diego rarely gets rain, never freezes, has an average annual daytime temperature between 58 and 70°F (15–21°C), and more than 70 miles (113km) of sandy beaches. California's second largest city, it retains a small-town ambience. Ralph Waldo Emerson must have visited San Diego when he said "California has better days and more of them."

What to See in San Diego

BALBOA PARK (➤ 16, TOP TEN)

59A2

THE BEACHES ✪✪✪

The most popular of the city's beaches is Pacific Beach (known as "PB" by the locals), which features The Tourmaline Surfing Park, a surfer's paradise. Mission Beach has a 3-mile (5-km) walk of shops and skateboard, rollerblade and bicycle rental stands. Ocean Beach is one of the liveliest in San Diego, and a good place to fish. Point Loma is an upscale beach, with spectacular views of the naval ships' comings and goings.

59A1
10 miles (16km) west of I-8 on Catalina Boulevard
619/557 5450
Daily 9–5.15
Inexpensive

CABRILLO NATIONAL MONUMENT ✪✪

A 144-acre (58-ha) park along steep cliffs, Cabrillo rewards with great views of San Diego Bay, and it's an especially good place to spot gray whales migrating to Mexico between mid-December and mid-March. The Old Point Loma Lighthouse, dating from 1855, is 25 miles (43km) out to sea, but visible from here on a clear day.

59B1
Visitor Center at 1100 Orange Avenue
619/236 1212

CORONADO ISLAND ✪✪✪

A combination of wealthy enclave and naval base, Coronado sits just across the bay from downtown San Diego. The easiest way to reach it is on the Bay Ferry.

SAN DIEGO
Scripps Oceanography and Birch Aquarium
Los Angeles
Miramar Naval Air Station
San Diego Wild Animal Park
0 5 km
Point La Jolla
La Jolla Caves
La Jolla Museum of Contemporary Art
UNIVERSITY CITY
3
LA JOLLA
Soledad Natural Park
San Clemente Canyon
NORTH CLAIREMONT
TIERRASANTA
JACOB DEKEMA FREEWAY
SAN DIEGO FREEWAY
5
805
52
163
15
274
Montgomery Field
San Diego
CLAIREMONT
SERRA MESA
PACIFIC BEACH
Tecolote Canyon Natural Park
CABRILLO FREEWAY
GRANTVILLE
MISSION BEACH
Mission Bay Park
LINDA VISTA
San Diego Stadium
Mission San Diego de Alcala
University of San Diego
8
2
Sea World
Mission Valley
Alvarado Canyon
Aztec Bowl
Old Town State Historic Park
OCEAN BEACH
Sports Arena
MIDWAY
Presidio Park
SAN DIEGO
Chollas Park
San Diego Int Airport
Balboa Park
San Diego Zoo
Museums
94
Sunset Cliffs Park
209
POINT LOMA
San Diego Bay
Maritime Museum
Gaslamp Quarter
ENCANTO
Seaport Village
North Island US Naval Air Station
Embarcadero
MONTGOMERY FREEWAY
1
CORONADO
CORONADO BAY BRIDGE
Cabrillo National Monument
NATIONAL CITY
LINCOLN ACRES
San Diego Bay
75
Tijuana, Mexico
A
B
C

Leaving from Broadway Pier downtown, the ferry arrives at Old Ferry Landing in Coronado in 15 minutes. You can also reach the island via the towering San Diego–Coronado Bay Bridge (toll). The main attraction on the island is Hotel Del Coronado (➤ 102). A testament to the beauty of Victorian architecture, the "Del" was opened in 1888, and film buffs might remember it as one of the main locations

☎ 619/437 8788 (Visitor Center), 619/234 4111 (Bay Ferry information)

Inexpensive

The Victorian-style Hotel del Coronado

GASLAMP QUARTER (► 62)

59B1
Balboa Park
619/234 0739
Sun, 2nd and 4th Tue of month
Free; donations welcome

HOUSE OF PACIFIC RELATIONS

The culture and art of 31 nations is housed in the museum's 15 California/Spanish-style cottages located in the Pan American Plaza. Other Plaza attractions are the Aerospace Museum, San Diego Automotive Museum and the open-air Starlight Bowl.

59A3
10 miles (16km) north of San Diego via I 805 or Highway 1

LA JOLLA

Pronounced *La Hoya* (Spanish for "The Jewel") this picturesque cove must surely be one of the prettiest places in the whole state. Just north of San Diego proper, it is considered the best place to examine marine life in a wild environment. This unspoiled piece of coastline offers expensive restaurants and boutiques on its two main thoroughfares: Prospect Street and Girard Avenue. Just north of La Jolla are the equally scenic towns of Del Mar and Solana Beach. Relatively undiscovered by tourists, these beaches epitomize the beauty and tranquillity of Southern California.

The crystal clear waters at La Jolla

59B1
1306 North Harbor Drive
619/234 9153
Daily 9–8 (closes 9 in summer)
Moderate

MARITIME MUSEUM OF SAN DIEGO

Basically just three ships are moored on the Embarcadero but oh, what legendary ships they are! The pick of the bunch is the 1863 *Star of India*, a fully equipped three-mast sailing ship, the oldest iron-hulled ship in America still afloat. San Francisco's *Berkeley* was the ferry used to evacuate victims of the 1906 earthquake. The 1904 steam-powered yacht *Medea* still occasionally sails around the Bay.

Mission San Diego de Alcala was Serra's first mission in California

Did you know ?

The California Tower carillon has no bells, but rather hammers bang against separate metal strips slightly larger than coat hangers.

MISSION BAY PARK ✪✪

There are miles of cycling paths throughout this huge aquatic park, and a bicycle rental stand can be found just off East Mission Bay Drive. Kite flying and volleyball are popular pastimes here, and just about anything to do with the water, as well as golf, picnicking and camping, can be found. The park is also the home of Sea World (▶ 64), and for many families the main reason for coming here. Just next to the park is Fiesta Island, popular with the locals for jet skiing and the curious game of "over the line" baseball.

- 59A2
- Daily
- Free
- 2688 E Mission Bay Drive
  - 619/276 8200

MUSEUM OF MAN ✪✪

The San Diego Museum of Man, located below the California Tower, offers eclectic, ever-changing exhibits from Californians and Hopi tribes, ancient Egypt and mummies, to Mayas and early man (▶ 16).

- 59B1
- Balboa Park
- 619/239 2001
- Daily 10–4.30
- Inexpensive

OLD TOWN SAN DIEGO STATE HISTORIC PARK ✪✪✪

The remains of the first European settlement in California, Old Town is preserved with National Park status. The most important area of Old Town is the Mission San Diego de Alcala, California's first mission, founded in 1769 by Father Junípero Serra. Restored and still used for services, it has beautiful gardens and adobe structures and houses the Museum de Luis Jayme. One of the oldest buildings, Casa de Estudillo, has survived several hundred years.

Old Town Plaza was a general meeting place and center for festivals, religious celebrations and even bullfights in the mid-1800s. Here you'll find the visitors' center where you can sign up for free tours of the grounds.

- 59B2
- San Diego Avenue, at Twiggs Street
- 619/220 5422
- Daily 10–5, closed Jan 1, Thanksgiving, Christmas Day
- Free

A Walk Around San Diego

Distance
3.5 miles (5.5km)

Time
3 hours

Start point
Visitors' Center, Old Town State Historic Park
59B2

End point
Old Town Plaza
59B2

Lunch
Casa de Bandini ($)
2754 Calhoun Street
619/297 8211
Sun–Thu 11–9, Fri–Sat 11–9.30

Starting at the Old Town visitors' center, you pass historic buildings, museums and sites that encompass the oldest and most beautiful part of San Diego.

From the visitors' center, walk southward and turn east on San Diego Avenue, continuing to the Machado-Silvas Adobe house.

This is one of the more famous buildings built in the mid-19th century, and houses the Courthouse and the Colorado House/Wells Fargo Museum.

After touring the house, continue a short distance north to Mason Street.

Here you will see the Mason Street School. Built in 1865, this one-room building was San Diego's first publicly owned school.

Go north on Mason to San Diego Avenue, then turn east to Dodson's Corner.

Dodson's Corner is a group of false-front shops where merchants sometimes dress in period costume. Across San Diego Avenue is the San Diego Union Museum, home of the state's longest running newspaper.

From here go north on Twiggs Street to Calhoun Street.

At Calhoun you will see the Steelly Stables, and Blackhawk Smith and Stable, both worth a look.

Walk west on Calhoun to the Alvarado House and Johnson House, two beautiful and historic structures. Retrace your steps back to Mason Street, then head south to visit the Casa De Estudillo. After touring the Casa, step across the street back into Old Town Plaza to end your tour.

To complement your stroll through Old Town, you could visit the nearby Gaslamp Quarter, bound by Broadway, 4th, 6th and Harbor streets, which gives a comprehensive history of San Diego's architecture.

Street art in the Gaslamp Quarter

PRESIDIO PARK ✪✪

Formerly the fort here protected Mission San Diego de Alcala. The park is up the hill from the center of Old Town. As you sit on the benches scattered among the trees of this 50-acre (20-ha) park you will have wonderful views of the Old Town expanse. San Diego's landmark museum, the Junipero Serra, sits high atop the hill where California's first mission and presidio were founded. Spanish, Mexican and Native American aspects of San Diego's history are recalled with exhibits of furniture, clothing, household items and other artifacts of the past 200 years.

- 59B2
- 2727 Presidio Drive
- 619/297 3258
- Park daily; Junipero Serra Museum daily 10–4.30
- Moderate

Rhinos at San Diego Wild Animal Park, Escondido

SAN DIEGO WILD ANIMAL PARK ✪✪

The park, 30 miles (48km) northeast of San Diego, is known for its authentic re-creation of African and Asian terrain. Almost 2,500 endangered animals are presented here by the Zoological Society of San Diego. This 2,100-acre (850-ha) preserve features a monorail tour, Nairobi Village animal shows, hiking trails and botanical exhibits.

- 69E1
- Via Rancho Pkwy exit off I-15
- 619/234 6541
- Daily 9–4
- Expensive (combination pass with San Diego Zoo)

SCRIPPS OCEANOGRAPHY AND BIRCH AQUARIUM ✪✪

Part of the University of California at San Diego, Birch Aquarium and the Memorial Pier are landmarks of the La Jolla coast. Marine scientists have been working here since the turn of the century. The Institute displays the aquatic world in indoor tanks, an on-shore tidepool and through additional oceanographic exhibits showing the latest advances in oceanography.

- 59A3
- 2300 Expedition Way
- 858/534 3474
- Daily 9–5
- Moderate

www.seaworld.com
- 59B2
- Sea World Drive off the I-5, Mission Bay Park
- 619/226 3901;
- Daily from 10am, closing times vary with season
- Expensive

SEA WORLD ✪✪✪

Perhaps one of, if not *the* finest marine biology park in the world, Sea World is impressive, and you can and should plan on spending the better part of a day here. Comfortably spread out over 150 acres (61ha), it features continuous killer whale and dolphin shows, and highly informative marine life exhibits. Between shows, you can touch or view live animals in the petting pools. Also not to miss are the nautical theme playground, marina and state-of-the-art research laboratories.

Sea World is home to killer whales Shamu and Baby Shamu, the real stars of the park, as well as seals, sea lions and walruses. The Rocky Point Preserve is a habitat for dolphins and sea otters, while "Penguin Encounter" has over 300 penguins. Other exhibits include "Pets Rule!" and "Fools with Tools." A family-oriented theme park features interactive games and adventures. Guided tours are available, and in the summer there are evening aquatic shows. Owing to the park's popularity, you can expect long waits for some shows and exhibits, especially during the summer.

Don't forget the re-entry stamp should you decide to leave the park and return later. Ticket sales stop 90 minutes before closing, which is around sunset most of the year, but up until 11pm in the summer.

Sea World deserves a whole day to do it justice

A Drive From San Diego

This drive includes historic Route 1, the Palomar Observatory and the San Diego Wild Animal Park.

Leave downtown on Route 1, going north out of the city. Pass through La Jolla.

Stop to enjoy the view from the cliffs (► 60). Also recommended is a stop at Torrey Pines State Preserve, a 1,000-acre (405-ha) area which has one of the world's two surviving stands of the Torrey pine tree. The walking trails are unique and offer a pleasant break from driving.

Continue north through Del Mar (stop at the famous racetrack if you are here in the summer), and on to Solana Beach, and finally Carlsbad.

Carlsbad is one of many pleasant communities in Southern California and is a good place to stop for lunch and do some shopping.

Highway 1 now becomes Interstate 5, which you follow north to SR 78. Exit and proceed east on SR 78 through San Marcos and into Escondido.

Champagne Boulevard in Escondido (10–5) is the world's only combined winery and car museum, with over 100 American convertibles on display.

Distance
60 miles (97km)

Time
About 5–7 hours, depending on time spent at attractions

Start/end point
Downtown San Diego
59A3

Lunch
Coyote Bar and Grill ($)
300 Carlsbad Village Drive
760/729 4695
Sun–Thu 11-10, Fri–Sat 11–11

A fine photo opportunity at San Diego Wildlife Park

From Escondido take SR 17 east to the San Diego Wild Animal Park (► 63). Spend a few hours here before continuing on SR 17 to Ramona. At Ramona take the junction on to Highway 67, a beautiful route that takes you past the Barona Indian Reservation. It then becomes the 8 Freeway, returning to downtown San Diego.

Rest of California

With its diverse environments and cultures, and its progressive way of thinking, California is more like an independent country than a state. As unique and varied as the major cities are, the outlying regions are even more so. There are the sprawling green vineyards of Napa and Sonoma valleys, the giant trees of Yosemite, Redwood and Sequoia national parks, mountains, deserts, inland seas and, of course, the ocean. The communities themselves range from upscale urban centers like Palm Springs to unpretentious farming and manufacturing towns. The 21 mission communities are perhaps the most charming of all. Their distinctive architectural style features stone and adobe, with whitewashed mud plaster inside and out. The pitched roofs of hewn timber, covered with red tiles, bring elegance and historical import to the entire state.

"... wonderful, wonderful, sublime, indescribable, incomprehensible; I never saw anything so truly and appallingly grand; it pays me a hundred times over for visiting California."

P. T. BARNUM
after his first visit to California

View from the Sky Jump at Knotts Berry Farm, Anaheim

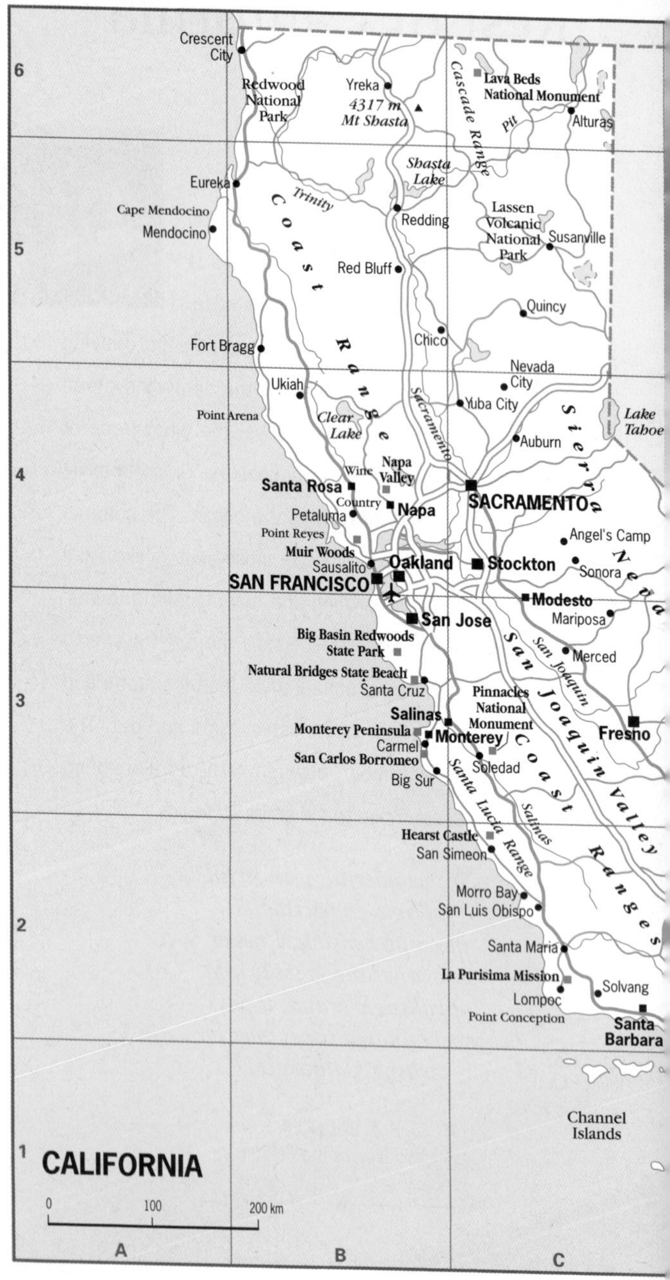

CALIFORNIA
Crescent City
Redwood National Park
Yreka
4317 m Mt Shasta
Cascade Range
Lava Beds National Monument
Pit
Alturas
Shasta Lake
Eureka
Trinity
Cape Mendocino
Mendocino
Redding
Lassen Volcanic National Park
Susanville
Red Bluff
Coast Range
Quincy
Chico
Fort Bragg
Nevada City
Ukiah
Sacramento
Yuba City
Point Arena
Clear Lake
Lake Tahoe
Auburn
Sierra Nevada
Wine Country
Napa Valley
Santa Rosa
Napa
SACRAMENTO
Petaluma
Point Reyes
Angel's Camp
Muir Woods
Sausalito
Oakland
Stockton
Sonora
SAN FRANCISCO
Modesto
Mariposa
San Jose
Big Basin Redwoods State Park
San Joaquin
Merced
Natural Bridges State Beach
Santa Cruz
Pinnacles National Monument
San Joaquin Valley
Salinas
Monterey Peninsula
Monterey
Fresno
Carmel
San Carlos Borromeo
Soledad
Big Sur
Santa Lucia Range
Salinas
Coast Ranges
Hearst Castle
San Simeon
Morro Bay
San Luis Obispo
Santa Maria
La Purisima Mission
Solvang
Lompoc
Point Conception
Santa Barbara
Channel Islands
0
100
200 km
A
B
C
1
2
3
4
5
6

OREGON
IDAHO
UTAH
NEVADA
Mono Lake
Yosemite National Park
Mammoth Lakes Rec Area
Devil's Postpile
Bishop
Scotty's Castle
Ubehebe Crater
Kings Canyon National Park
Independence
4418 m Mt Whitney
Sequoia National Park
Devil's Golf Course
Death Valley
3368m
Visalia
Delamo
Bakersfield
Ridgecrest
Mojave Desert
Ghost Town of Calico
Barstow
Colorado
Needles
Lancaster
Six Flags Magic Mountain
Lake Arrowhead
Sonora Desert
Big Bear Lake
Ventura
Simi Valley
Pasadena
San Bernardino
ARIZONA
Oxnard
LOS ANGELES
Anaheim
Joshua Tree National Monument
Palm Springs
Blythe
Riverside
Long Beach
Disneyland
Salton Sea
San Juan Capistrano
Catalina Island
Mount Palomar
Oceanside
Escondido
Brawley
La Jolla
SAN DIEGO
D
E
MEXICO
F

What to See in the Rest of California

69D1
46 miles (74km) from Los Angeles via I–5; directly across from Disneyland

ANAHEIM

Anaheim was originally founded as the center of a wine-producing colony by German immigrants in 1857. The vineyards were replaced by orange groves late in the 19th century, after an especially brutal drought. Oranges thrived until the 1950s, when commercial interests and the rapid growth of the Los Angeles metropolitan area took over. The two main attractions in the area are Disneyland Park (➤ 18) and Knott's Berry Farm (➤ 78).

69D2
California Living Museum
10500 Alfred Harrell Highway
661/872 2256
Tue–Sun 9–5
Picnic facilities
Inexpensive

Kern County Museum
3801 Chester Avenue
661/852 5000
Mon–Sat 10–5, Sun noon–5
Moderate

BAKERSFIELD

Bakersfield is California's main oil-producing center. Many consider it a less-than-desirable part of California, its furnace-like, 100°F-plus summers a major drawback. However, the downtown area is a vital mix of restored buildings and newer offices. Of note in the town are a genuine schoolhouse, church and a fully restored 1868 log cabin.

The **California Living Museum** focuses on the state's wildlife and native plants, many of which have become rare or endangered.

Kern County Museum has exhibits representing both human and natural history of the area.

69E2
Calico Ghost Town
11 miles (18km) northeast of Barstow via I-15
760/254 2122
Daily 9–5
Restaurants moderate
Moderate

Rainbow Basin National Natural Landmark
Fossil Bed Road, 8 miles (13km) north of Barstow via SR 58

BARSTOW

Barstow is the halfway point between Los Angeles and Las Vegas. Settled in the early 19th century, silver mines flourished in the surrounding areas. The town of **Calico** boomed in the late 1800s, and its mines produced $15 million worth of ore. When the price of silver dropped, the town went bust. Today, you can visit the "ghost town" of Calico to pan for gold, ride the steam railway or see a show at the Calikage Playhouse.

North of Barstow is **Rainbow Basin National Natural Landmark**, formed by the deposit of sediment over millions of years. Fossils, the forces of nature and an abundance of minerals give it its dramatic shapes and colors.

69E2
Big Bear Chamber of Commerce, 630 Bartlett Road
909/866 4607
Many restaurants ($–$$$)

BIG BEAR LAKE

One of California's largest recreation areas, the Big Bear Lake region has two distinct sections; Big Bear Lake and Big Bear City, on the eastern end of the lake. Big Bear Village, centered around the lake, is popular for lodging, dining and shopping. Camping, hiking and horse-back riding are available in summer and skiing in winter.

CARMEL ✪✪✪

Carmel was established in the late 19th century and has since gained its reputation as a bohemian retreat. It has some of the most picturesque coastal residences in the state, many in Spanish-Mission style. **Mission San Carlos Borromeo del Rio Carmelo** (1769) was moved to its riverside site here in Carmel in 1771. Father Junípero Serra is buried in the church, which was given the status of minor basilica by the Pope in 1960.

68B3

Mission San Carlos Borromeo del Rio Carmelo

3080 Rio Road

831/624 1271

Mon–Fri 9.30–4.30, Sat, Sun 10–30–4.30

Free, but donations accepted

Left: *Mission San Carlos Borromeo del Rio Carmelo, final resting place of Junípero Serra*

Below: *Bicycling at Big Bear Lake*

CATALINA ISLAND (➤ 16, TOP TEN)

DEATH VALLEY NATIONAL PARK ✪✪✪

Three million years ago, inner-earth forces tormented, twisted and shook the land in what is now Death Valley, creating snowcapped mountains and superheated valleys. Lakes, formed during the Ice Age, evaporated, leaving alternating layers of mud and salt deposits.

More than three million acres in size, Death Valley ranges in elevation from 282ft (86m) below sea level to slightly over 11,000ft (3,354m) above. Temperatures reach well over 100°F (38°C) in summer, making it one of the hottest regions in the world. **Scotty's Castle**, on the northern boundary of the park, is a Spanish/Moorish construction built by Chicago insurance tycoon Albert Johnson for Walter E. Scott, alias "Death Valley Scotty."

69E3

Furnace Creek Visitors Center

760/786 3244

Daily 8–5

Some areas disabled accessible

Inexpensive

Camping facilities

Scotty's Castle

760/786 2392

Daily 8.30–5.30

Moderate

The beautiful Blossom Trail in the fruit orchards around Fresno

EUREKA

Eureka is the largest town on California's northernmost coast. Set along Humboldt Bay, it is home to an impressive fishing fleet. Its name, from the Greek word for "I have found it," refers to the cries from many gold miners (called '49ers) in the 19th century. The Old Town section is worth a visit for its elegantly refurbished Victorian homes.

The old 1912 building, once the town's main bank, now houses the **Clarke Memorial Museum**. It houses an excellent collection of California Native American historic artifacts.

Blue Ox Millworks is a working mill that includes a blacksmith shop and a re-creation of a logging camp. **Sequoia Park,** a beautiful grove of virgin redwoods in 52 acres (21ha), has a formal flower garden, duck pond, and deer and elk paddocks.

68B5

Clarke Memorial Museum
Third and "E" streets
707/443 1947
Tue–Sat 11–4
Free

Blue Ox Millworks
Foot of "X" street
707/444 3437
Mon–Fri 9–5, Sat by appointment
Inexpensive

Sequoia Park
Glatt and "W" Streets
707/442 6552
Daily 10am–dusk
Picnic facilities
Inexpensive

FRESNO

Fresno lies in the heart of the San Joaquin Valley. One of the foremost agricultural areas in the country, it is also the gateway to the Sierra Nevada's three national parks.

The town's fine **Metropolitan Museum of Art, History and Science** features an extensive collection of Asian art, as well as American still-life paintings. Wild Water Adventure Park, on E Shaw Avenue, contains over 20 water rides, pools and a small fishing lake.

68C3

Metropolitan Museum of Art, History and Science
1555 Van Ness Avenue
559/441 1444
Tue–Sun 11–5
Inexpensive

GOLD COUNTRY TOWNS

Also known as the Mother Lode Country, this scenic area extends 300 miles (484km) along Highway 49, through the western Sierra Nevada foothills. Once the thriving Old West, it is now mostly ghost towns, several of which are open to tourists.

Angel's Camp Museum, in Angel's Camp (➤ 74), was the center for gravel and quartz mining in 1849. You can see photographs, relics and 3 acres (1.2ha) of old mining equipment from the old days.

68C4

Angel's Camp Museum
753 South Main Street
209/736 2963
Mar–end Dec daily 10–3; Jan–end Feb Sat, Sun 10–3
Inexpensive

Marshall Gold Discovery State Historic Park is where James Marshall discovered gold. The drive-through park features a replica of Sutter's Mill and memorial statue and grave site of James Marshall.

The Empire Mine State Historic Park (➤ 74), 2 miles (3.5km) east of Grass Valley, is the Gold Country's best preserved quartz mining operation. During the boom years, the 367 miles (592km) of mine shafts produced six million ounces of gold.

Mercer Caverns, 1 mile (1.6km) north of Murphys, via Main Street, were discovered in 1885 by Walter Mercer, a gold prospector. The 45-minute tour gives the opportunity to view the enormous stalagmites and stalactites close up.

Marshall Gold Discovery State Historic Park
- North fork of the American River and Highway 49, Coloma
- 530/622 3470
- Museum daily 10–3; park 8–sunset
- Inexpensive

JOSHUA TREE NATIONAL MONUMENT ✪✪✪

Known for its distinctive Joshua trees (a desert tree of the yucca species), and its uniquely shaped rock formations, the park connects the "high' and 'low" deserts. In the park is Key's View, a high elevation with incredible views on a clear day. Not to be missed is the Cholla Cactus Garden, about 10 miles (16km) south of the Oasis Visitors Center.

- 69E1
- Oasis Vistors Center, National Monument Drive, 29 Palms
- 760/367 5500
- Daily 8–5
- Inexpensive

Did you know ?

UFO devotees insist there is a secret starship base hidden somewhere in the brush-dotted hills of the park at Joshua Tree. At Giant Rock Airport (2477 Belfield, off Reches Road and Highway 247, Yucca Valley) you can visit a mysterious 40-ft (12-m) dome, Integration, a showpiece for UFO cultists.

The striking Joshua tree is said to be so named because Western pioneers believed it resembled the biblical Joshua raising his arms to the heavens and stopping the sun so the Israelites could win their battle

A Drive Through the Gold Country

Gold was discovered in Jamestown in 1848

This drive will take you through Gold Country along historic Highway 49.

Begin in Mariposa, where SR 49 meets SR 140.

Here you can visit the California State Mining and Mineral Museum and the Mariposa County Museum.

Proceed north on SR 49 to Chinese Camp and the State Historic Park. A few miles north is Jamestown.

Jamestown served as a backdrop for the film *High Noon* and the television series *Little House on the Prairie.*

Follow 49 north, stopping in Tuttletown.

You can view a replica of Mark Twain's cabin on Jackass Hill (Tuttletown was originally called Jackass Gulch).

Continue to Columbia.

Here you can try your hand at panning for gold, or ride an authentic stagecoach.

Continue north on 49 to Angel's Camp.

This is where Mark Twain first heard the "jumping frog" story from bartender Ben Coon. If you are here in May, don't miss the frog jumping contest. The foundation of Angel's Mine, one of the region's most profitable, can be found across from the Catholic Church.

Continue north to Jackson and Placerville.

Jackson was once home of the Mohawk Indians, and Placerville was formerly known as "Hangtown." Gold Bug Mine is worth a visit.

Further north are Coloma, Auburn and Grass Valley.

The latter is home to Empire Mine State Historic Park (➤ 73) and North Star Mine Museum, both offering tours.

The drive ends in Nevada City.

Distance
Approximately 100 miles (161km)

Time
8 hours

Start point
Mariposa
68C3

End point
Nevada City
68C4

Lunch
National Hotel Restaurant ($)
18183 Main Street, Jamestown
209/984 3446

LAKE ARROWHEAD ✪✪

Known locally as a sophisticated mountain getaway, this is where LA's wealthy spend leisurely weekends in luxury homes. Restrictive development laws help preserve the area's natural beauty. Swimming and boating are popular activities in summer, and skiing in winter.

69E2
Chamber of Commerce, Lake Arrowhead Village
909/337 3715
Mon–Fri 9–5, Sat 10–3

LAKE TAHOE ✪✪✪

Situated on the California–Nevada stateline, Lake Tahoe is one of the most popular resort communities in the state. Although this beautiful lake is 6,228ft (1,899m) above sea level, it never freezes because of its depth. You will find top-notch ski areas here, and in summer, water sports include lake cruises, water skiing and sailing.

For a spectacular aerial view of the entire area, including the site of the 1960 Winter Olympic Games, ride the gondola to the top of the Squaw Valley Ski Area.

68C4
Squaw Valley Cable Car
1960 Squaw Valley Road, Olympic Valley
530/583 6985
Call to check. Closed mid Oct–Dec 1
Moderate

Bumpass Hell, at Lassen

LASSEN VOLCANIC NATIONAL PARK ✪✪✪

Lassen Park stretches over 100,000 acres (40,486ha) in the northeastern corner of California, where the Cascade and Sierra Nevada mountains meet. Highlights are Lassen Peak, Cinder Cone, Prospect Peak and Mount Harkness, the latter two volcanoes topped by cinder cones.

Lassen's numerous volcanic eruptions subsided in 1921 and have been replaced by inviting hot springs and lakes, lava flows and mudpots, all linked together by hiking trails that lead to the summit and back.

68C5
9 miles (15km) east of Mineral, via SR 36
530/595 4444
Year-round

MAMMOTH LAKES RECREATION AREA ✪✪

This giant popular resort area in the Inyo National Forest has world-class skiing, and in summertime it's a mountain biking mecca. There is also good camping, fishing and horseback riding here. Hike to the 101-ft (31-m) Rainbow Falls, or visit the Devil's Postpile National Monument, 60-ft (18-m) multi-sided columns that are by-products of former volcanic activity.

69D3
Chamber of Commerce, PO Box 123, Mammoth Lakes, 93546
760/934 3068
Mon–Fri 9–5
Restaurants ($$)

MENDOCINO 

Mendocino, off scenic US 1, is perhaps the most charming small town in California. It is noted for its Cape Cod and Victorian-style architecture and its active, artistic community. The entire town is on the National Register of Historic Places. Film buffs will recognize it from such films as *The Summer of '42, East of Eden* and television's *Murder She Wrote*.

The **Art Center** is the epicenter of the many art museums in the community, and includes galleries, live theater and arts and craft fairs.

Mendocino Chamber of Commerce
- 68A5
- 332 North Main Street
- 707/961 6300
- Daily 11–4

Mendocino Art Center
- 45200 Little Lake Street
- 707/937 5818 or 800/653 3328
- Call for times
- Moderate

MODESTO 

This quintessential California town was made famous by George Lucas's film *American Graffiti*. Near the center of the state, it is the home of the Blue Diamond Almonds company.

The **McHenry Museum** re-creates a 19th-century school, blacksmith shop, kitchen, country store and others with changing exhibits. The **McHenry Mansion**, a block away, exhibits antique furnishings and artwork in a restored Victorian home.

- 68C4

McHenry Museum & Mansion
- 1402 "I" Street
- 209/577 5366 (museum); 577 5341 (mansion)
- Tue–Sun noon–4. Closed major holidays
- Free, donations requested
- Tours of mansion offered Sun–Thu 1–4, Fri noon–3

MONTEREY PENINSULA (➤ 22, TOP TEN)

MORRO BAY 

Morro Rock, the conical, volcano-shaped rock that towers 578ft (176m) out of the Pacific Ocean, sits guarding the entrance to Morro Bay, which is known primarily for its commercial fishing and oyster farming. Although the town has a modest tourist trade, the locals are mostly concerned with the daily business of fishing. Beneath the rock stretches a 5-mile (8-km) long beach with 85-ft (26-m) high white sand dunes that serve as a habitat for bird and plant life.

The Morro Bay Arts Festival takes place each weekend in October, and the **Museum of Natural History** exhibits marine life native to the central coast, including the Bay's sea lions. **Tiger's Folly Cruises** offers harbor cruises.

The State Park, south of Morro Bay, is beautiful and a must for those who enjoy camping and hiking. The campgrounds are at the southern end of the park surrounded by cypress and eucalyptus.

The Galley Restaurant serves delicious seafood meals.

- 68C2
- 845 Embarcadero Road, Suite D
- 805/772 4467
- Mon–Fri 8.30–5, Sat 10–4
- Free

Museum of Natural History
- Morro Bay State Park
- 805/772 2694
- Daily 10–5
- Inexpensive

Tiger's Folly Cruises
- 1205 Embarcadero
- 805/772 2257
- Call for schedules
- Inexpensive

MOUNT PALOMAR ✪✪✪

Palomar Observatory houses the world-famous 200-in (513-cm) Hale telescope. High above the distracting, bright city lights, the observatory also has several smaller telescopes, used to monitor the planet's movement. The small Greenway Museum contains photographs of the observatory's celestial sightings.

- 69E1
- 4.5 miles (7km) north of San Diego on SR 6
- 626/395 4033
- Daily 9–4
- Free

MOUNT SHASTA ✪✪

Spiritual-minded Californians flock to this mountain because it is said to be a "vortex of spiritual energy." For the more earthbound there is hiking, climbing, and skiing in winter. Several surrounding lakes offer waterside camping, fishing and watersports, including skating in winter.

The **Mount Shasta State Fish Hatchery**, in the center of the area, produces 5 to 10 million trout annually to stock Northern California lakes.

- 68B6
- Chamber of Commerce Visitors Bureau, 300 Pine Street
- 800/926 4865

Mount Shasta State Fish Hatchery

- 530/926 2215
- Daily 7am–dusk
- Free

OAKLAND ✪✪

Linked to San Francisco by the Bay Bridge, Oakland has long suffered from its close proximity to the city across the bay. In reality, it is a culturally rich and diversified town and has counted among its famous citizens Jack London and Gertrude Stein. **Oakland Museum** has an extensive collection of historical and contemporary art housed in the Gallery of California Art. The museum is one of the best in the state for studying the diverse cultural make-up and subsequent historical progress.

Lake Merritt, created in the late 19th century by the damming of a section of the Oakland estuary, was one of the first natural wildlife preserves established in the US.

- 68B4

Oakland Museum

- 11th and Oak Street
- 510/238 2200
- Wed–Sat 10–5, Sun noon–5
- Inexpensive

Mount Shasta is usually snow-capped all year

Orange County

Known by Californians as the "conservative" enclave of the state, Orange County is a sprawling, seemingly endless expanse of humanity between Los Angeles and San Diego, with its own unique charms.

DISNEYLAND PARK (➤ 18, TOP TEN)

FESTIVAL OF THE ARTS/PAGEANT OF THE MASTERS

- Off map 47E1
- Laguna Canyon Road, Laguna Beach
- 949/494 1145
- Jul–end Aug 10am–11pm
- Expensive

A state-of-the-art art exhibit in the scenic wooded Laguna Canyon, this is a landmark event, the former featuring an exhibit of 150 Laguna artists of all kinds. The most interesting aspect of this seven-week event, however, is the Pageant of the Masters, in which human models stand perfectly still for three minutes in re-creations of famous paintings and sculptures, with a musical accompaniment.

HUNTINGTON ART CENTER

- 47D1
- 538 Main Street E, Huntington Beach
- 714/374 1650
- Wed–Sun noon–6, Sun noon–4
- Free

Though small, the Huntington Art Center is concerned with local contemporary art and architecture in a big way. It has been renovated and is a favorite with many local artists. Films are shown the first and third Friday of each month.

INTERNATIONAL SURFING MUSEUM

- 47D1
- Olive Street
- 714/960 3483
- Summer daily noon–5; winter Thu–Mon noon–5
- Inexpensive

Huntington Beach calls itself "Surf City," with good reason, and is a mecca for surfing enthusiasts. Exhibits tell the sport's history, and the store sells surf gear, all, of course, to the music of the Beach Boys.

KNOTT'S BERRY FARM

- 47E2
- 8039 Beach Boulevard, Buena Park
- 714/220 5200
- Subject to change; call for current times
- Expensive

One of California's original theme parks, Knott's has grown from a true berry farm to a modern 150-acre (61-ha) attraction with over 165 rides. The Western theme areas include Ghost Town and Gold Mine Ride. Other attractions include Camp Snoopy, Wild Water Wilderness, Mystery Lodge, Reflection Lake, California Marketplace and Kingdom of the Dinosaurs. For the adventurous, there are four awesome rollercoasters, the Boomerang, Montezooma's Revenge, the Jaguar and the Silver Bullet. And, finally, for the truly hungry, Knott's serves its original, delicious, world-famous boysenberry pie.

LAGUNA ART MUSEUM

- Off map 47E1
- Pacific Coast Highway and Cliff Drive, Laguna Beach
- 949/494 8971
- Daily 11–5
- Moderate

The Laguna Art Museum was founded in 1918 and is the showcase venue for the Laguna Art Association. It usually features several visiting exhibits of paintings and sculpture by California artists. On permanent display are historical California landscapes and vintage photographs of the region.

MISSION SAN JUAN CAPISTRANO ✪✪✪

Founded in 1776, this is one of California's most beautiful missions, and the only building still standing where Father Serra said mass. On 19 March each year, the Feast of St. Joseph celebrates the legendary "return of the swallows."

- 69D1
- Cnr of Ortega Highway/ Camino Capistrano
- 949/234 1300
- Daily 8:30–5

Mission San Juan Capistrano, the seventh of the California missions

Did you know ?

The swallows of San Juan Capistrano have the reputation of returning every March 19. In reality, they return over a period of several weeks. They leave their winter home in South America around October 23 on their 6,000-mile (9,677-km) flight home to spend spring and summer in Southern California.

SHERMAN LIBRARY AND GARDENS ✪✪

The unique gardens here are filled with orchids and koi ponds, while the library itself is a large building, taking up a whole city block. It functions as a center of historical research for the region. There is an extensive collection of historical Orange County documents and photographs.

- Off map 47E1
- 2647 E Coast Highway, Newport Beach
- 949/673 2261
- Gardens daily 10.30–4
- Inexpensive

YORBA LINDA ✪✪

The **Richard Nixon Presidential Library and Birthplace**, in Yorba Linda, has galleries, theaters and gardens, and personal memorabilia of this former US president. The grounds feature the small house where he was born, his post-presidency private study and a re-creation of the White House's Lincoln Sitting Room.

- 47F2
- 18001 Yorba Linda Boulevard
- 714/993 3393
- Mon–Sat 10–5, Sun 11–5.
- Moderate

In the Know

10

Ways to Be a Local

Dress casual but trendy. Sunwear and exercise clothes in the south; alternative wear in San Francisco; hiking boots and jeans in the north.

Carry a cellular phone and/or handheld device.

In Los Angeles, talk about movie deals.

In San Francisco, talk about the fog.

In San Diego and the desert areas, don't talk, just smile in a laid-back manner.

Absolutely no one walks in Los Angeles, so rent a convertible, or better still, a Mercedes convertible.

Eat light and healthy meals like salads, tofu and fresh fruit, accompanied by a glass of Californian wine.

Safeguard yourself and your valuables. In major cities, lock your car doors while driving. At the beaches, don't carry your wallet in your back pocket.

California-speak is as casual as the lifestyle, and often includes a Mexican word or two. Say Ro-DAY-oh (Rodeo), Si-PUL-vi-dah (Sepulveda), and La Con-YAH-dah (La Cañada). But don't worry if you slip into your native tongue, you hear almost every language in the world here.

Carry a bottle of water with you at all times; "foreign" water is the "coolest."

Good Places To Have Lunch

Gladstones 4 Fish ($$)
Fresh seafood on the beach.
17300 Pacific Coast Highway, Pacific Palisade, Los Angeles 310/GL4 FISH, 310/454 3474

The Tea Pavillion ($$)
Great views in Balboa Park accompanied by sushi, Japanese noodles and specialty teas.
Balboa Pk, San Diego
619/231 0048

Ceviche—a popular seafood dish

Pinks Hot Dog Stand ($)
Grunge stand with limo parking and great dogs and burgers.
Highland and Melrose, Los Angeles

Clementine ($)
Breakfast/lunch café near Century City.
1751 Ensley Avenue, Los Angeles 310/552 1080

Karl Strauss' Old Columbia Brewery & Grill ($$)
Specialties are burgers, fresh fish and German-style sausage. Watch the microbrewery process while you sip a cold one.

✉ 1157 Columbia Street, San Diego ☎ 619/234 2739

Dottie's True Blue Café ($)
Lunch/breakfast choices. ✉ 552 Jones Street, San Francisco ☎ 415/885 2767

Gabriella Café ($$)
Californian/Italian cuisine. ✉ 910 Cedar Street, Santa Cruz ☎ 831/457 1677

Pier 23 Café ($$)
✉ The Embarcadero (Pier 23) at Broadway, San Francisco ☎ 415/362 5125

Tarpy's Roadhouse ($$)
Steak, seafood and American comfort food. ✉ 2999 Monterey-Salinas Highway, Monterey ☎ 831/647 1444

Fat City Café and Bar ($–$$)
Art nouveau, old European atmosphere with stained glass and a 100-year-old bar. Light entrées and rich desserts. ✉ 1001 Front Street, Sacramento ☎ 916/446 6769

10 Top Activities

- **Surfing**
- **Exercising** at a gym or health club, or by doing yoga, pilates or ta'i chi
- **Hiking/backpacking**
- **Going to the movies**
- **Cycling**
- **Rollerblading**
- **Boating** (all kinds)
- **Golfing**
- **Going to the** theme parks
- **Attending concerts** from rock to jazz to classical

10 Unique Annual Events

- National Date Festival and Fair (camel and ostrich races), Indio, February (☎ 760/863 8247)
- Snowfest (West's largest), Tahoe City, March (☎ 530/546 5253)
- Mendocino/Fort Bragg Whale Festival, March (☎ 707/961 6300)
- Frog Jumping Contest, Angel's Camp, May (☎ 209/736 2561)
- Dixieland Jazz Jubilee, Sacramento, May (☎ 916/372 5277)
- Great Monterey Squid Festival, Monterey, May (☎ 831/649 6544)
- Gilroy Garlic Festival, Gilroy, July (☎ 408/842 1625)
- Grand National Rodeo, Horse, and Stock Show, Daly City (world-class), October (☎ 415/404 4100)
- Doo Dah Parade (spoof of famous Rose Parade), Pasadena, November (☎ 626/440 7379)
- Monarch butterfly migration to Pismo Beach's Butterfly Trees, November to March

10 California Specialties

- Sit-ins
- Sun and surf
- San Francisco hippies
- Spiritual seekers
- Sonoma and Napa Valley wines
- Stars (human, not celestial)
- Smog
- Smoking prohibitions
- San Andreas fault
- Sequoias

Rafting on the Stanislaus River

OXNARD ✪

Oxnard is a harbor town located on the Ventura–Los Angeles county line, and is home to an annual Strawberry Festival each May. Surpisingly overlooked by visitors are the 7 miles (11km) of beautiful beaches lining the town.

The **Carnegie Art Museum** has a permanent collection of 20th-century California painters, while changing exhibits feature photography and sculpture, with some shows spotlighting local artists.

The **Ventura County Gull Wings Children's Museum**'s hands-on exhibits of fossils and minerals, including a puppet theater and make-believe campground, will entertain the kids.

69D2

Carnegie Art Museum
- 424 S "C" Street
- 805/385 8157
- Thu–Sat 10–5, Sun 1–5
- Inexpensive

Ventura County Gull Wings Children's Museum
- 418 W 4th Street
- 805/483 3005
- Tue–Sat 10–5
- Inexpensive

PALM SPRINGS ✪✪✪

Rising out of the desert like on oasis, Palm Springs is one of the most famous resort towns in the world. It has become a favorite of wealthy retirees with a penchant for good golf and bad driving habits, and an ever-increasing number of young people are looking here for a brief spring retreat from their studies. The summers are insufferably hot, however, and the population dwindles from June through early September.

Anza-Borrego Desert State Park offers spectacular desert scenery. Set in 600,000 acres (242,915ha), the park's main flora includes lupine, poppy, dune primrose, desert sunflower and desert lily. A variety of short trails and camp-grounds can be found here.

Five miles (8km) south of Palm Springs is **Agua Caliente Indian Reservation**. The Tribal Council here has opened part of the reservation for hiking and picnics.

An awesome view of the San Jacinto Mountains awaits if you ride the **Palm Springs Aerial Tramway**, almost 5,000ft (1,524m) straight up. The perfect way to escape the debilitating summer heat, you ride up to the wooded trails and campgrounds at the top, where refreshments are available.

69E1

Anza-Borrego Desert State Park
- Visitors Center, 2 miles (3.2km) west of Borrego Springs Township
- 760/767 5311
- Call for hours and more information
- Inexpensive

Agua Caliente Indian Reservation
- 760/323 0151
- Wed–Sat 10–5, Sun noon–5 (shorter hours in summer)
- Inexpensive

Palm Springs Aerial Tramway
- Tramway Road, 3 miles (5km) southwest of SR 111
- 760/325 1391
- Mon–Fri 10–8, Sat–Sun 8–8. Closed 2 weeks in Aug
- Expensive

Resident of the Agua Caliente Indian Reservation

PETALUMA

Petaluma is another one of the quintessential small California towns. Situated on the Petaluma River, it has retained most of its 19th-century architecture and, like Modesto (➤ 76), has become a favorite for filming television series and movies.

Philanthropist Andrew Carnegie endowed $12,500 toward the construction of the **Historical Museum/Library** in 1903. It houses permanent and rotating exhibits of early 19th-century Petaluma.

68B4

Petaluma Historical Museum/Library
20 4th Street
707/778 4398
Wed–Sat 10–4, Sun noon–3
Inexpensive

REDWOOD NATIONAL PARK (➤ 25, TOP TEN)

RIVERSIDE

Because the region has the ideal climate and soil for growing navel oranges, this was the wealthiest US city per capita and the metropolitan center of Southern California at the turn of the century. Several buildings remain from around this time: the Italian Renaissance-style City Hall, the Classic Revival municipal museum, and many exquisite Victorian homes. In addition, mission architecture and adobe residences still reflect the early wealth and prestige.

California Citrus State Historic Park features a grove of 80 varieties of citrus trees. The visitor center is a Victorian house typical of the city's heyday era. The Riverside Municipal Museum, at 3720 Orange Street, traces the history of citrus-growing in the region.

69D1

California Citrus State Historic Park
Van Buren Boulevard at Dufferin Avenue
951/780 6222
Daily 8–5 (until 7 Apr–Sep); visitor center Wed, Sat, Sun 10–4
Picnic facilities
Free

Palm Springs Aerial Tramway

The carefully restored State Capitol Building, centre of California's government

68C4

Governor's Mansion State Historic Park
- 16th and "H" streets
- 916/323 3047
- Daily 10–4
- Inexpensive

Spirit of Sacramento
- Old Sacramento's "L" Street Landing
- 916/552 2933
- Cruises: lunch, brunch, happy hour, dinner, sunset and sightseeing
- Dinner, brunch and happy hour cruises available
- Moderate

Discovery Museum
- 101 "I" Street
- 916/264 7057
- Summer daily 10–5; winter Tue–Sun 10–5
- Inexpensive

California State Railroad Museum
- Second and "I" streets
- 916/445 6645
- Daily 10–5
- Moderate

State Capitol
- Between 10th, 15h, "L" and "N" streets
- 916/324 0333
- Tours daily 9–4
- Free

Sutter's Fort
- 27th and "L" streets
- 916/445 4422
- Daily 10–5
- Inexpensive

Sacramento Zoo
- 3930 Westland Park Drive
- 916/2264 5885
- Daily 9–4 (10–4 Nov–end Jan)
- Moderate

SACRAMENTO

Sacramento was once a major supply center for the California '49ers (gold seekers); now it is the state capital. The names of 5,822 Californians killed in the Vietnam War are engraved on the 22 black granite panels of the California Vietnam Veterans Memorial, near the State Capitol Park.

The exquisite **Governor's Mansion** dates from the 1800s and is now a museum of Victoriana. Items from former governors include a 1902 Steinway piano and Persian carpets.

The Historic Paddlewheeler ***Spirit of Sacramento*** is available for a Sacramento River cruise or special events. The boat's murder-mystery trips on the *Spirit* are especially popular.

A million-dollar gold collection, ethnic photos and a historic print shop are just some of the items in the five separate areas of the **Discovery Museum**. The **California State Railroad Museum** has three entire floors devoted to railroad-related exhibits, including train cars and 21 locomotives.

Noted for its 210-ft (64-m) dome, the **State Capitol** building is nearly 150 years old, and is open daily for tours. Adobe-style **Sutter's Fort** was the first European outpost in California and contains some interesting period relics.

Sacramento Zoo has a large reptile display and 350 species of wild animals.

The Towe Ford Museum and Waterworld USA (► 111) are also worth visiting.

SALINAS ✪

John Steinbeck was born in this working-class town 17 miles (27km) inland from Monterey, now home to the National Steinbeck Center. While it's sometimes overlooked in favor of its more affluent neighbors, Salinas is charming. For those visiting in August, there is the Steinbeck Festival. Many rodeo fans visit the town in July to catch one of the major stops on the professional rodeo circuit.

The ***Hat In Three Stages of Landing*** is a unique giant sculpture by Claes Oldenberg which captures a trio of bright yellow hats, each weighing 3,500lb (1,590kg). The sculpture graces the lawn of the Community Center where there are art exhibits and musical/theatrical performances.

68B3

National Steinbeck Center
1 Main Street
831/796 3833; www.steinbeck.org
Daily 10–5, closed major holidays
Moderate

SAN JOSE ✪✪

San Jose is the 11th largest city in the US. It was founded in the last quarter of the 18th century as El Pueblo de San Jose, and is the oldest Spanish civilian settlement. From 1849 to 1851 it served as the state's capital.

Kelley Park, apart from being a popular city park with such attractions as Happy Hollow family play area and zoo, also contains the Japanese Friendship Garden and Teahouse and the San Jose Historical Museum.

Babylonian, Sumerian and Assyrian artifacts, mummies, sculptures and more can be found at the **Rosicrucian Egyptian Museum and Planetarium**. There is also a contemporary art gallery.

The **Winchester Mystery House**, a Victorian mansion and home of eccentric firearms heiress, Sarah Winchester, was designed to confuse evil spirits. The layout of the house is so complex, with blind closets, secret passageways, 13 bathrooms and 40 staircases, that even Sarah herself needed a map to find her way around. Over looking the Santa Clara Valley from the 4,209-ft (1,283-m) summit of Mount Hamilton is the **Lick Observatory.**

68B3

Kelley Park
Senter and Story roads
Daily 8 to 30 minutes before dusk
Picnic facilities
Inexpensive

Rosicrucian Egyptian Museum and Planetarium
1342 Naglee Avenue
408/947 3636
Mon–Fri 10–5, Sat–Sun 11–6
Moderate; senior/student rates

Winchester Mystery House
525 S Winchester Boulevard
408/247 2101
Daily from 9am, closing times vary with time of year
Expensive

Lick Observatory
Mount Hamilton Road
408/274 5061
Mon–Fri 12.30–5, Sat–Sun 10–5
No nearby food or auto services
Free

The bizarre Winchester House—a maze but well worth the tour price

69E1

Bowers Museum of Cultural Art
2002 N Main Street
714/567 3600
Tue–Sun 11–4
Inexpensive

SANTA ANA 

A typical thriving small city in Orange County, Santa Ana centers around the South Coast Plaza, a European-styled mall with shops, restaurants and cinemas. The **Bowers Museum of Cultural Art**, a mission-style museum, is the largest in Orange County. It focuses on American, Pacific and African art, with an impressive permanent collection and quarterly visiting exhibits.

Mission Santa Barbara, often called the Queen of the Missions

68C2
El Presidio de Santa Barbara State Historic Park
122–129 E Canon Perdido Street
805/965 0093
Phone for opening hours
Free

Mission Santa Barbara
E Los Olivos and Laguna Street
805/682 4149
Daily 9–5; closed major holidays
Inexpensive, under 16 free

Museum of Art
1130 State Street
805/963 4364
Tue–Sun 11–5
Moderate. Free Sun

SANTA BARBARA 

A pleasant and affordable day trip from Los Angeles by train (moderate cost) taking you along the Pacific coast in the morning, gives you time to explore the historic adobes and museums. Lunch on Stearns Wharf, explore the specialty shops there, then stroll the white-sand beach, or play a short round of golf before returning in late afternoon. The County Courthouse, on Anacapa Street, is one of the best examples of Spanish-Moorish architecture in the US.

El Presidio de Santa Barbara State Historic Park, on the site of a late-1700 Spanish outpost, includes historical buildings such as El Cuartel, the second-oldest surviving edifice in California.

Mission Santa Barbara is the best preserved of the 21 California missions, and the church is filled with Mexican art from the 18th and 19th centuries. A Moorish fountain from 1808 graces the front and the mission is the site of The Little Fiesta each August.

The **Santa Barbara Museum of Art** has a wide variety of American, Asian and 19th-century French, Greek and Roman antiquities, including a major photographic collection.

Visit the Zoological Gardens which are natural habitats for 600 animals, and feature over 80 exhibits.

SIMI VALLEY ✪✪

The main reason for visiting Simi Valley is to see the **Ronald Reagan Presidential Library**, set in a beautiful, Spanish mission-style, hilltop mansion. Among the exhibits are photographs and memorabilia of the former US president's life, a full-scale replica of the Oval Office and a large portion of the Berlin Wall.

69D2
Ronald Reagan Presidential Library
40 Presidential Drive
800/410 8354
Daily 10–5; closed major holidays
Inexpensive

SOLEDAD ✪

Soledad, the oldest settlement in the Salinas Valley, was established in 1791 with the founding of **Mission Nuestra Señora de la Soledad**, 3 miles (5km) west on US 101. The ruins of this adobe mission, along with a restored chapel and museum, can be seen to the east of town.

68C3
Mission Nuestra Senora de la Soledad
Fort Romie Road
831/678 2586
Daily 10–4
Donations

SOLVANG ✪✪✪

Denmark in California might best describe Solvang, with its Danish architecture, windmills, gaslights and cobblestone walks. A tour of Solvang is possible in a horse-drawn Danish streetcar, and the town hosts several remarkable festivals annually. Contrasting the Scandinavian motif is the **Old Mission Santa Ines**, founded in 1804.

68C2
Chamber of Commerce, 1693 Mission Drive
805/688 0701 or 800/468 6765
Scandinavian restaurants and cafés ($–$$$)

Old Mission Santa Ines
1760 Mission Drive
805/688 4815
Summer 9–6, Oct–end May 9–5.30; closed major holidays
Inexpensive

Typical Solvang architecture

VENTURA ✪

This small beach town between Los Angeles and Santa Barbara is worth a brief visit.

San Buenaventura Mission was founded in 1782. The church is restored and the museum exhibits Native American artifacts from the Chumash tribes.

Albinger Archaeological Museum displays over 3,500 years of remains, all from areas around the Mission, while Ventura County Museum of History and Art has Native American, Hispanic and pioneer exhibits.

69D2

San Buenaventura Mission
211 East Main Street
805/643 4318
Mon–Fri 10–5, Sat 9–5, Sun 10–4; closed major holidays
Inexpensive

68B4

Napa Valley Visitors Bureau

1310 Napa Town Center, Napa 94559

707/226 7459

Hours vary; some tours require reservations

Sonoma Valley Visitors Bureau

453 1st Street, E Sonoma

707/996 1090

Daily 9–5

Napa Valley Wine Train

707/253 2111 or 800/427 4124

Year-round

Expensive, reservations and deposit required

THE WINE COUNTRY

North of San Francisco lie some of the most lush valleys in all of California, the best known of which are the Napa (➤ 24) and Sonoma Valleys. It is here that California's vintners tend their grape vines and produce the many varied wines known and enjoyed world-wide. Whether you are driving, bicycling, taking the Wine Train or flying over the area in one of the many hot air balloons that offer spectacular views of the verdant, rolling, wine lands, you will never forget your excursion to the Wine Country.

The estates of the wineries are incredible to see. Take one of the guided tours of the processing facilities with their informative, enticing tastings. While the large wineries are the most popular, don't pass up the small, family-owned ones, of which there are many. Most have wines that rival the greats, with more convivial atmospheres.

The Napa Valley Wine Train provides daily excursions through the Napa Valley. The 1917 Pullman Dining Car relives the gracious era of elegant rail travel and distinguished service and makes you feel as if you're riding the Orient Express as the three-hour, 36-mile (58-km) trip between Napa and St. Helena allows for a leisurely brunch, lunch or dinner. Many concerns are aired by residents that the wineries are a bit too commercial for the area, but there are rarely complaints from the visitors.

Above: *Reaping the rewards of a perfect climate.* Opposite: *Harvesting grapes in Alexander Valley, Sonoma*

To the west, the Sonoma Valley runs for 15 miles (24km) and is a bit less populated than the Napa Valley. As a rule, the 30 or so wineries here offer more personalized tours, with free tastings and a more relaxed atmosphere. The town of Sonoma itself is a good place to start if you wish to visit the valley. The other center of activity is Santa Rosa, to the north of the region.

The Sonoma Valley is particularly rich in Spanish and Mexican history, so be sure to take note of the area's beautiful architecture.

If you're looking for souvenirs of your visit to California, the on-site gift shops have unique offerings and superb wines they will ship anywhere in the world. The wineries listed are just some of the ones you'll want to explore. *Spotlight's Wine Guide* is a complete guide to the area (☎ 415/898 7908).

BERINGER VINEYARDS

Beringer was one of the very first wineries to open its cellar doors to visitors. The staff here are especially attentive and knowledgeable in discussing the process of wine making and its history. There are regular tours throughout the day.

Just north of downtown St. Helena, 2000 Main Street
707/963 7115
Hours and tours vary, phone for information

BUENA VISTA WINERY

As the site of the first vineyard in the valley, Buena Vista, 2 miles (3km) northeast of Sonoma, has become a historical landmark. The wine cellars, built in 1857, are the oldest stone cellars in the state. The Tasting Room offers selection of award-winning wines and there is a gift shop, a picnic area, an artists' gallery, self-guided tours and historical presentations.

18000 Old Winery Road
707/938 1266
Daily 10–5

KENWOOD VINEYARDS

Operating on Jack London's former ranch since 1970, this Sonoma country winery produces Cabernet Sauvignon, Zinfandel, Sauvignon Blanc, Chardonnay, Gewürztraminer, Merlot and Pinot Noir on the estate which is about 1-hour's drive north of San Francisco. Visitors can sample up to four wines, which are produced from grapes grown on site and sourced from local vineyards, and can hike and take bicycle rides around the property.

9592 Sonoma Highway (Highway 12), Kenwood
707/833 5891
Daily 10–4.30

Did you know?

Over a century ago, Hungarian Agoston Haraszthy planted the first vineyard in California, near the small town of Sonoma, seeding it with the best European grapes he could find. The state gave him funding, but neither envisioned the huge industry that would spring from his venture.

A Walk in Sequoia National Park

Distance
5 miles (8km)

Time
2–4 hours

Start point
General Sherman Tree
69D3

End point
General Sherman or Long Meadow
69D3

Lunch
Grant Grove Restaurant ($$)
Grant Grove Visitors Center
559/335 5500, ext 306

This walk takes you through the forest of Sequoia National Park. Even if you visit during the heat of the summer, you will find the temperatures comfortably cool because of the towering foliage.

Begin at the General Sherman Tree, 2 miles (3.2km) east of Giant Forest Village.

The General Sherman tree (named for the Civil War general) is 275ft (84m) high. It is estimated to be more than 2,500 years old and contains enough wood to build 40 houses.

Walk down the self-guided, paved Congress Trail. Cross Sherman Creek on the quaint wooden bridge.

Experience the awesome giant sequoias, like the character-laden Leaning Tree and some lightning-struck and fire-scarred trees as well.

Whole groves of giants florish in Sequoia

About a mile (1.6km) further, you will meet the junction with the Alta Trail and a grove known as The Senate. A little further along the fern-filled trail is The House Grove.

These two stands are named after the two governing bodies of the United States government. The path also visits the McKinley Tree (named for the US president). After World War II, the practice of naming big trees after politicos was abandoned.

Continue a half-mile (0.8km) back, and return to the trail head. For a longer hike (about 6 miles/10km), follow the Congress Trail to the junction of The Trail of the Sequoias. Take this path for a half-mile (0.8km) to the hike's high point, then gradually descend one and a half miles (2.5km) into Long Meadow.

Lunch before, or after, your hike at Giant Forest Village.

Where To...

Above: *City Lights bookstore, North Beach*
Right: *Fisherman's Wharf is the place to go for fresh seafood in San Francisco*

San Francisco

Prices
Average meal per head excluding drink:
$ = up to $15
$$ = between $15 and $30
$$$ = over $30

Good Old Dishes
The local cuisine of San Francisco dates back to the Gold Rush days. Old faithful dishes such as cioppino (seafood casserole), hangtown fry (oysters dipped in egg and flour and fried with bacon), fortune cookies and Irish coffee are among the most famous. Most fresh fish is grilled with a bit of Slavic, or French, influence.

Diamond Ratings
AAA tourism editors evaluate and rate each restaurant on the overall quality of food, sevice, decor and ambience—with extra emphasis given to food and service. Ratings range from one diamond indicating a simple family-oriented establishment to five diamonds indicating an establishment offering superb culinary skills and an ultimate dining experience.

Alfred's ($$)
Quintessential steakhouse with bordello-like setting. Portions to suit big appetites.
659 Merchant Street, between Kearny and Montgomery streets 415/781 7058 Lunch, dinner

Aqua ($$$)
Glamorous downtown restaurant serving French-American gourmet seafood.
252 California Street 415/956 9662 Lunch, dinner

Balboa Cafe ($$)
Trendy café with a traditional American menu. The place to "see and be seen."
3199 Fillmore Street 415/921 3944 Lunch, dinner

Betelnut ($$)
Lively atmosphere, tropical drinks and pan-Asian fare, with elements of Thai, Chinese and Korean cuisine.
2030 Union Street 415/929 8855 Lunch, dinner

Bix ($$$)
Martinis, cigar smoke, upscale crowd and great steaks and seafood make this one of San Francisco's most popular restaurants. Reservations recommended.
56 Gold Street, between Montgomery and Sansome streets 415/433 6300 Dinner; lunch Fri only

Caffe Sport ($$)
Italian restaurant, a favorite with North Beach regulars. Sicilian specialties.
574 Green Street 415/981 1251 Lunch, dinner; closed Sun, Mon; no credit cards

Le Charm ($$)
French bistro and garden with terrific prix fixe menu.
315 5th Street 415/546 6128 Lunch, dinner

Dottie's True Blue Cafe ($)
Great diner for typical American food. Home-style atmosphere and affordable prices make it a hit.
522 Jones Street 415/885 2767 Breakfast, lunch; closed Tue

Ebisu ($$)
Top-rated sushi and traditional Asian food. You may have to wait but its worth it.
1283 Ninth Avenue 415/566 1770 Lunch, dinner

Firefly ($$)
Local favorite for home cooking and friendly service. Great place to people watch.
4288 24th Street 415/821 7652 Lunch, dinner

Fleur de Lys ($$$)
The city's most romantic restaurant. Attentive service and superb contemporary French food.
777 Sutter Street 415/673 7779 Lunch, dinner; closed Sun

Fog City Diner ($$)
Upscale '50s-style diner on Telegraph Hill. American and seafood specialties.
1300 Battery Street 415/982 2000 Lunch, dinner

Gary Danko ($$$)
Romantic Russian Hill/wharf restaurant featuring French-Californian fare. Diners can design their own three- to five-course meal. Pricey, but worth it.

800 N Point Street 415/749 2060 Dinner only

The House ($$)
Quaint and quiet with superb food Asian-American cuisine at a moderate price.
1230 Grant Avenue 415/986 8612 Lunch, dinner

Jeanty at Jacks ($$)
Opened in 1864, this historic restaurant has a new owner and a new French menu.
615 Sacramento Street 415/693 0941 Lunch, dinner

Kate's Kitchen ($)
Authentic, inexpensive "soul" food in the famous Haight-Ashbury district. Great for breakfast or late-night dining.
471 Haight Street 415/626 3984 Breakfast, lunch, dinner; no credit cards

Lulu ($$)
Innovative, Mediterranean bistro located in a large converted warehouse. Family-style service with excellent food.
816 Folsom 415/495 5775 Lunch, dinner

The Mandarin ($$$)
Long-time favorite for great views and exotic environment. Chinese cuisine; specializes in Peking duck.
900 N Point Street 415/673 8812 Lunch, dinner

Mel's Drive In ($)
A revival of the popular 1950s-style drive-in. Top-rated burgers, fries and milk shakes and, of course, a great jukebox.
2165 Lombard Street 415/921 2867; 3355 Geary Street 415/387 2244; 801 Mission Street 415/227 4477 Lunch, dinner, open late

L'Osteria del Forno ($$)
Northern Italian cuisine in North Beach. Expect a long wait, as the restaurant is tiny and the food delicious.
519 Columbus Avenue 415/982 1124 Lunch, dinner; closed Tue; no credit cards

Perry's ($)
Local watering hole, so popular with the young set that they added a second location. Good American foodand a comfortable ambience.
1944 Union Street 415/922 9022; 185 Sutter Street 415/989 6895 Lunch, dinner

PlumpJack Cafe ($$)
"Hot spot" specializing in American food. Offers top-notch wine list. Reservations may be difficult to get, but you'll be glad you persisted.
3127 Fillmore Street 415/563 4755 Lunch, dinner

Slanted Door ($$$)
Creative Vietnamese food accompanied by a fantastic view of the Bay Bridge.
Ferry Building, 1 Ferry Plaza 415/861 8032 Lunch, dinner

Swan Oyster Depot ($$)
Unique seafood emporium in operation since 1912. Service from an old-fashioned marble bar.
1517 Polk Street 415/673 1101 Lunch, dinner; closed Sun; no credit cards

Diversity
The strength of any great city is the diversity of its cuisine and restaurants. San Francisco certainly flexes its muscles in this respect. The most elegant restaurants are located in the center of the city. By region, the best Italian can be found in the North Beach area, while Latin dishes are the highlights in the Mission District. Chinatown offers Asian restaurants, naturally, from Thai to Vietnamese to Cambodian.

Los Angeles

Ethnic Mix
Los Angeles restaurants reflect the city's diverse ethnic mix. Tail-o-the-Pup hot dog stand (San Vicente & Beverly) combines architectural uniqueness with a great dog, and just a couple of blocks away, La Cienega Boulevard's "restaurant row" offers eateries for every taste and budget. Because smoking is prohibited in Los Angeles County restaurants and the weather is gorgeous year-round, patio dining is nouvelle vogue.

Apple Pan ($)
A throwback to the 1940s (authentic) this LA institution serves fresh, juicy hamburgers, tasty fries and pie at a burger counter.
10801 W Pico Boulevard 310/475 3585 Lunch, dinner; closed Mon

Border Grill ($$)
Hip cantina by the beach. Serves exotic Mexican specialties. Stylish ambience; great margaritas.
1445 4th Street, Santa Monica 310/451 1655 Lunch, dinner

Buffalo Club ($$$)
Westside club/restaurant, with top-notch American cuisine.
1520 Olympic Boulevard (at 15th Street) 310/450 8600 Lunch, dinner

Café Talesai ($$)
Fresh and natural ingredients at this hip Thai place, located in a mall. Try the hidden treasures signature appetizer.
9198 Olympic Boulevard 310/271 9345 Lunch Mon–Fri, dinner daily

Cheesecake Factory ($)
One of the most popular restaurants in Southern California because of its huge portions of traditional American fare and a gauntlet of cheesecake.
364 N Beverly Drive, Beverly Hills 310/278 7270 4142 Via Marina, Marina del Rey 310/306 3344 Lunch, dinner

Dan Tana's ($$$)
Long-time celebrity hangout for Italian food, the best steaks and fresh lobster. *Very* Hollywood.
9071 Santa Monica Boulevard 310/275 9444 Dinner only, but open late

Duke's ($)
Sunset Strip coffee shop/diner where fantastic omelettes attract the young and hip. Long lines at breakfast, especially on weekends.
8909 Sunset Boulevard 310/652 3100 Breakfast, lunch, dinner

El Cholo ($$)
Long-established family-owned Mexican serving traditional fare since 1927. Another location is in Santa Monica.
1121 S Western Avenue 323/734 2773 Lunch, dinner

The Ivy ($$$)
Great American food and the place to see and be seen in LA. Outdoor patio. To ensure a table reservations are a must.
113 N Robertson Boulevard 310/274 8303 Lunch, dinner

Lawry's Prime Rib ($$$)
The best for prime rib anywhere, supposedly, in the world. "To die for," says one. You decide, but make reservations early.
100 N La Cienega 866/223 8224 Dinner only

Maple Drive ($$$)
Well-known Beverly Hills celebrity-owned restaurant. American menu and pleasing jazz.
345 N Maple Drive, Beverly Hills 310/274 9800 Lunch, dinner; closed Sun

Matsuhisa ($$$)
The flagship restaurant of the growing Nobu empire, Matsuhisa serves fantastic sushi and sashimi in a bustling, intimate setting.
129 N La Cienega 310/659 9639 Lunch Mon–Fri, dinner daily

Musso and Frank ($$)
A touch of "Old Hollywood" serving traditional fare. Great martinis and the best Caesar salad in LA.
6667 Hollywood Boulevard 323/467 7788 Lunch, dinner; closed Sun, Mon

L'Orangerie ($$$)
Modern-classic French food. Impeccable service; terrace dining. Consistently in California's top listings. Dress code.
903 N La Cienega Boulevard 310/652 9770 Dinner only; closed Sun, Mon

Pacific Dining Car ($$$)
Downtown standard for steaks and seafood. Draws day-time business crowd but is best in the evening. Reservations recommended.
1310 W 6th Street 213/483 6000 Breakfast, lunch, dinner

Parkway Grill ($$)
The continental cuisine is worth the trip to Pasadena. Also California fare.
510 S Arroyo Parkway, Pasadena 626/795 1001 Lunch Mon–Fri, dinner daily

Patina ($$$)
Comfortable and unpretentious French bistro.
141 S Grand Avenue 213/972 3331 Lunch, dinner

Roscoe's House of Chicken and Waffles ($)
Famous with locals for its informal setting, sinfully greasy chicken and delectable waffles any time of day. Several locations.
1514 N Gower Street (at Sunset Boulevard) 323/466 7453 Breakfast, lunch, dinner, open late

Spago ($$$)
World-renowned for chef Wolfgang Puck's gourmet pizzas, and its star-studded Academy Awards party. Also fine California cuisine.
176 N Canon Drive 310/385 0880 Dinner only

Surya India ($$)
Samosas, tandoori and curries near the farmers' market.
8048 W 3rd Street 323/653 5151 Lunch, dinner

Tommy's Original Hamburger ($)
Perhaps the greatest hamburger stand on the planet. Greasy, but great!
2575 Beverly Boulevard 213/389 9060 Daily 24hrs; no credit cards

Trattoria Farfalla ($)
Italian café serving great thin-crust pizzas. Usually crowded, but worth the wait.
1978 N Hillhurst Street, Los Feliz 323/661 7365 Lunch, dinner

Valentino ($$$)
Elegant, expensive Italian, with a great wine list and impeccable service. Reservations required.
3115 Pico Boulevard, Santa Monica 310/829 4313 Dinner; lunch only on Fri; closed Sun

People-watching
California was at the forefront of the coffee-house and health food restaurants craze. It is also the state where "hanging out" and "people-watching" have been elevated to an art form. Sunset Plaza (West Hollywood), Ventura Boulevard (San Fernando Valley), La Brea (Hollywood), Melrose Avenue (Hollywood), and the beaches in Venice, Santa Monica and Malibu are exceptional areas to go when you wish to sit, feed and watch.

San Diego

Whatever You Choose
San Diego's restaurants are known for their emphasis on seafood and South-of-the-Border cuisine. The Downtown, Old Town and Hillcrest sections offer the most diverse choices of dining and ambience. Other areas that offer cafés, coffee-houses, diners and fine dining are Ocean Beach, Point Loma, Coronado, Mission Beach and Pacific Beach. The San Diego area also has a great many health food and vegetarian restaurants.

Anthony's Star of the Sea Room ($$$)
Family-owned seafood restaurant. Great service, beautiful harbor views. Jacket required.
1360 Harbor Drive 619/232 5103 Lunch, dinner

Athens Market ($$)
No-frills Greek restaurant. Belly dancers on weekends.
109 W F Street 619/234 1955 Lunch Mon–Fri, dinner daily

Cafe Lulu ($)
Coffeehouse/restaurant in the Gaslamp Quarter neighborhood. One of the few late-night places to eat.
419 F Street 619/238 0114 Breakfast, lunch, dinner; no credit cards

Café Pacifica ($$)
Good seafood specialties in unique, old cemetery setting.
2414 San Diego Avenue, Old Town 619/291 6666 Dinner only

City Delicatessen ($)
Centrally located Jewish deli.
535 University Avenue 619/295 2747 Breakfast, lunch, dinner, open late

Dakota ($)
Mesquite-grilled fish and fowl at good prices. Live music.
901 5th Avenue 619/234 5554 Lunch Mon–Fri, dinner daily

Dick's Last Resort ($)
Continental dining in a converted warehouse.
345 Fourth Avenue 619/231 9100 Lunch, dinner

Le Fontainebleau ($$$)
Expensive French restaurant in The Westgate Hotel. Offers gallery of original oil paintings and award-winning seafood and veal. Pianist.
1055 Second Avenue 619/557 3655 Lunch, dinner

Hob Nob Hill ($$)
Family-owned and open since World War II. Specialties include fried scallops and rack of lamb. Kids' menu.
2271 First Avenue (near Balboa Park) 619/239 8176 Lunch, dinner

Kansas City Barbeque ($)
No-frills barbecue stand with lots of personality.
610 W Market Street 619/231 9680 Lunch, dinner

Old Town Mexican Cafe ($)
This café is the place for the best Mexican fare in San Diego.
2489 San Diego Avenue 619/297 4330 Breakfast, lunch, dinner

Rainwaters on Kettner ($$$)
Private club atmosphere with standard American cuisine. Dress code enforced.
1202 Kettner Boulevard 619/233 5757 Lunch, dinner; no lunch on weekends

Thee Bungalow ($$)
This family-run French spot has seen pleasing restaurant loyalists for over 30 years.
4996 West Point Loma Boulevard 619/224 2884 Dinner daily

Umi Sushi ($$)
Traditional sushi offerings, plus tempura, teriyaki and specials.
2806 Shelter Island Drive 619/ 226 1135 Lunch Mon–Sat, dinner daily

Rest of California

Eureka

Sea Grill ($$)
Extensive seafood menu that includes cod Louisiana and Hawaiian mahi-mahi.
316 "E" St, Old Town 707/443 7187 Lunch, dinner. Closed Sun

Marin County

Olema Farm House Restaurant ($$)
This shingle-sided eatery was a stagecoach stop in 1872, but today's fare is nouveau American.
10005 Highway 1, Olema 415/663 1264 Breakfast, lunch, dinner

Mendocino

Mendocino Hotel ($$$)
Cozy, antique-filled hotel. Dine in an elegant Victorian parlor or garden café. Excellent Continental cuisine and seafood specialties.
45080 Main Street 707/937 0511 Breakfast, lunch, dinner

Montecito

Montecito Cafe ($$)
California cuisine; warm setting in The Montecito Inn.
1295 Coast Village Road 805/969 3392 Lunch, dinner

Stonehouse ($$$)
Regional cuisine in rustic, romantic setting. At the San Ysidro Ranch Resort.
900 San Ysidro Road 805/969 5046 Lunch, dinner

Morro Bay

Hoppe's ($$)
International cuisine and great wine list.
78 North Ocean Avenue 805/772 9012 Lunch, dinner; closed Mon–Tue

Ojai

Suzanne's Cuisine ($$)
A real gem off the beaten path. Inexpensive California cuisine.
502 W Ojai Avenue 805/ 640 1961 Lunch, dinner; closed Tue

Ranch House ($$)
A lush garden patio, with meat and seafood dishes.
W Lomita Avenue 805/646 2360 Dinner Tue–Sun, Sun brunch

Orange County

Antonello Risorante ($$)
A local favorite serving Northern Italian fare in an elegant setting.
3800 Plaza Drive, Santa Ana 714/751 7153 Lunch Mon–Fri, dinner Mon–Sat

Aubergine ($$$)
Classic French cuisine on the Balboa peninsula. Elegant atmosphere.
508 29th Street, Newport Beach 949/723 4150 Dinner only; closed Mon

Bistango ($$)
Combined restaurant and art gallery with Continental cuisine, prix fixe. Extensive wine list and nightly entertainment.
19100 Von Karman Avenue, Irvine 949/752 5222 Lunch Mon–Fri, dinner daily

Cafe Zoolu ($$)
Funky and eclectic. Known for its vegetarian delights and grilled specialties.
860 Glenneyre Street, Laguna Beach 949/494 6825 Dinner only; closed Mon

Satisfying Your Needs
Food lovers will find California like no other place on earth in its diversity and sheer number of restaurants and cafés. California has initiated such US culinary trends as sushi bars, the buzz-word nouvelle and, naturally, California cuisine. Although Mexican and South American dishes are prevalent, you can satisfy just about any food craving in the Golden State.

Ocean Views
From San Diego to the top of the state, along California Route 1, you are guaranteed to find small inns with sweeping views of the Pacific and excellent food at moderate prices. Or, for funky fun and lots of food for little money, there are also the roadhouses, like the not-to-be-missed Patrick's in Santa Monica.

Clay Oven ($)
Delightful Indian restaurant with friendly service and great prices. Good lunch buffet.
15435 Jeffrey Road (Irvine Center), Irvine 949/552 2851 Lunch, dinner

Jack Shrimp ($$)
Spicy Cajun, casual environment; moderately priced.
2400 W Coast Highway, Newport Beach 949/650 5577 Lunch (Fri only), dinner

Javier's ($$)
Ocean views and large portions. Try the house specialty.
480 S Coast Highway 949/474 1239 Lunch, dinner

McCharles House and Tearoom ($$)
Superb Continental menu. Famous for its desserts. Unique Victorian décor, pleasant patio under huge eucalyptus trees.
335 S "C" Street, Tustin 714/731 4063 Call for opening times

Oysters ($$)
New and trendy place for fresh seafood and wine from the owner's vineyard. Live entertainment.
2515 E Coast Highway, Corona del Mar 949/675 7411 Dinner only

Stix ($$)
A budget Chinese restaurant offering fast but friendly service.
28251 Crown Valley Parkway, Laguna Niguel 949/831 7849 Lunch, dinner

Tangata ($$)
Continental and Southwestern cuisine in the Bowers Museum.
2002 N Main Street, Santa Ana 714/550 0906 Lunch only Tue–Sun

21 Ocean Front ($$$)
A charming seafood restaurant at the foot of Newport Pier.
2100 W Oceanfront, Newport Beach 949/673 2100 Dinner only

Zinc Café and Market ($)
Stereotypical California, vegetarian coffee-house. Great muffins. Hangout of the arty set. Usually crowded, but worth the wait.
350 Ocean Avenue, Laguna Beach 949/494 6302 Breakfast, lunch only

Zov's Bistro ($$)
Trendy, with Mediterranean cuisine and fresh bread from the on-site bakery.
17740 E 17th Street, Tustin 714/838 8855 Lunch, dinner

Palm Springs/Palm Desert

La Casuelas Terraza ($)
Mexican food and fantastic margaritas in a relaxing but lively atmosphere.
222 South Palm Canyon Drive, Palm Springs 760/325 2794 Lunch, dinner daily

Cedar Creek Inn ($$)
Home-town favorite for reliable American food.
1555 S Palm Canyon Drive 760/325 7300

Cuistot ($$$
A popular and elegant restaurant featuring

California-French cuisine. The specialties are veal and rack of lamb. Pricey but worth it.
72595 El Paseo, Palm Desert 760/340 1000 Lunch, dinner; closed Mon

Palm Springs Chop House ($$$)
Steaks, chops and large side orders, plus tasty desserts.
262 S Palm Canyon Drive 760/320 4500 Dinner only

Ristorante Mamma Gina ($$)
Authentic northern Italian with homemade pasta, chicken and veal specialties.
73–705 El Paseo Drive 760/568 9898 Lunch, dinner

San Luis Obispo

Big Sky Cafe ($)
Here you'll find Caribbean cuisine in a fun and casual environment.
1121 Broad Street 805/545 5401 Breakfast, lunch, dinner

Buono Tavola ($$)
A great-value Italian restaurant in a casual, country setting.
1037 Monterey Street 805/545 8000 Lunch Mon–Fri, dinner daily

Santa Barbara

Brophy Brother's Clam Bar and Restaurant ($$)
Spectacular views and an energetic crowd.
119 Harbor Way 805/966 4418 Lunch, dinner

Carlito's Cafe ($)
Budget Mexican and interesting vegetarian plates.
1324 State Street 805/962 7117 Lunch, dinner

Chucks of Hawaii ($$)
Polynesian décor and award-winning steaks and wine. Casual fun atmosphere.
3888 State Street 805/687 4417 Dinner only

Citronelle ($$$)
Ocean views welcome diners at this sophisticated restaurant. Interesting French and California cuisine.
901 Cabrillo Boulevard 805/963 0111 Lunch, dinner

The Hitching Post ($)
Barbecue, steaks and french fries in a casual roadhouse atmosphere.
406 E Highway 246, Buellton 805/688 0676 3325 Point Sal Road, Casmalia 805/937 6151 Dinner only

Wine Country

Bistro Don Giovanni ($$$)
Serves Italian and Mediterranean specialties in a beautiful artistic setting. Daily pasta specials.
4110 Howard Lane, Napa 707/224 3300 Lunch, dinner

French Laundry ($$$)
Thomas Keller's famed new French restaurant. Takes reservations months in advance. Outdoor dining area. Prices are very steep.
6640 Washington Street, Yountville 707/944 2380 Lunch, dinner daily

Mustards ($$)
Napa Valley's trendiest and most popular spot for California cuisine. Reservations recommended.
7399 St Helena Highway, St. Helena 707/944 2424 Lunch, dinner

Roadside Stands
To complement California's wide range of restaurants and cuisines, an abundance of roadside stands offer fresh-picked produce and fruit. There is no better way to sample the culinary diversity of a region, and whether you want a refreshing and healthy traveling snack or an inexpensive breakfast to enjoy in your room, you'll find these roadside wares excellent value.

San Francisco

Prices
You may expect to pay the following prices per room per night.
$ = under $100
$$ = between $100 and $250
$$$ = over $250

Diamond Ratings
AAA tourism editors evaluate and rate each lodging establishment based on the overall quality and services. AAA's diamond rating criteria reflect the design and service standards set by the lodging industry. combined with the expectations of its members.
A one or two diamond rating represents a clean and well-maintained property offering comfortable rooms, with the two diamond property showing enhancements in decor and furnishings. A three diamond property shows marked upgrades in physical attributes, services and comfort and may offer additional amenities. A four diamond rating signifies a property offering a high level of service and hospitality and a wide variety of amenities and upscale facilities. A five diamond rating represents a world-class facility, offering the highest level of luxurious accommodations and personalized guest services.

Archbishop's Mansion ($$)
Historic 1904 bed-and-breakfast with stained-glass windows and elegant European furnishings.
1000 Fulton Street
415/563 7872

Beresford Arms Hotel ($$)
A traditional hotel with Continental breakfast. Tea, wine and snacks in the afternoon. Near Union Square.
701 Post Street **415/673 2600** **Wheelchair access**

Comfort Inn by the Bay ($)
Near Lombard Street and the major attractions. Reasonable rates.
2775 Van Ness Avenue
415/928 5000
Wheelchair access

The Fairmont Hotel and Tower ($$$)
Newly renovated historic hotel, situated atop Nob Hill.
950 Mason Street **415/772 5000** **Wheelchair access**

Four Season's Clift ($$$)
This art deco hotel has Oriental carpets, chandeliers and tasteful rooms.
495 Geary Street
415/775 4700

Hotel Rex ($$$)
Near Union Square, in a style inspired by art and literary salons of the early 1900s.
562 Sutter Street
415/433 4434

Hotel Triton ($$)
Near Chinatown. Tasteful art deco design with exhibitions of local artwork in the lobby.
342 Grant Avenue
415/394 0500
Wheelchair access

The Inn at the Opera ($$$)
Near Performing Arts Center. Small and elegant with first-rate service.
333 Fulton Street **415/863 8400** **Wheelchair access**

Mark Hopkins Inter-Continental ($$$)
On the site of the old Mark Hopkins mansion. Offers a spectacular view of the city.
1 Nob Hill **415/392 3434**

Mill Valley Inn ($$)
Beautiful hotel central to this small, artistic community.
165 Throckmorton Avenue, Mill Valley **415/389 6608**

Queen Anne ($$)
Converted art deco style Victorian house. Complimentary breakfast, and afternoon tea and sherry; attentive staff.
1590 Sutter Street **415/441 2828** **Wheelchair access**

Sir Francis Drake ($$)
Opulence with bed-and-breakfast flavor.
450 Powell Street
415/392 7755

White Swan Inn ($$–$$$)
A boutique hotel in Nob Hill, with 26 rooms and a convenient location.
845 Bush Street
415/775 1755

York Hotel ($$)
Renovated 1922 hotel. Parts of Alfred Hitchcock's *Vertigo* were filmed here.
940 Sutter Street
415/885 6800

Los Angeles

The Argyle ($$$)
An LA landmark; 15 stories of art deco elegance at the end of Sunset Strip. Popular movie location.
✉ 8358 Sunset Boulevard, W Hollywood ☎ 323/654 7100

Beverly Hills Hotel ($$$)
Restored in the early 1990s by its owner, the Sultan of Brunei. Known for its private bungalows and the celebrity-packed Polo Lounge.
✉ 9641 Sunset Boulevard ☎ 310/276 2251

Chateau Marmont Hotel ($$$)
Favorite of film and music communities in the style of a Loire Valley château.
✉ 8221 Sunset Boulevard ☎ 323/656 1010

Holiday Inn($$)
Reliable accommadations from this international chain.
✉ 1020 S Fiqueroa St, Downtown LA ☎ 213/748 1291

Hollywood Roosevelt ($$)
Site of first Academy Awards presentation (1927). Centrally located (► 21).
✉ 7000 Hollywood Boulevard ☎ 323/466 7000

Hotel Bel-Air ($$$)
Exotic Mediterranean-style hotel. A hideaway for the rich and famous.
✉ 701 Stone Canyon Road ☎ 310/472 1211

Hotel Sofitel ($$)
Affordable Mediterranean-style hotel. Across from the Beverly Center Mall (► 107).
✉ 8555 Beverly Boulevard ☎ 310/278 5444

Malibu Beach Inn ($$$)
Mediterranean-style hotel on a white-sand shore.
✉ 22878 Pacific Coast Highway, Malibu ☎ 310/456 6444

New Otani Hotel and Garden ($$$)
Japanese-style hotel. Beautiful gardens, well-appointed rooms.
✉ 120 S Los Angeles Street ☎ 213/629 1200

Sheraton Universal ($$$)
Views of Hollywood Hills and San Fernando Valley. Close to Universal City attractions. Good-value weekend packages.
✉ 333 Universal Hollywood Drive Parkway ☎ 818/980 1212

Shutters on the Beach ($$$)
Contemporary beachfront hotel with all the amenities. Marble bathrooms, sweeping ocean views.
✉ 1 Pico Boulevard, Santa Monica ☎ 310/458 0030

Sunset Marquis ($$$)
Mediterranean décor, mostly suites. Set on a residential street, this hotel is a favorite of the entertainment community for its casual atmosphere.
✉ 1200 N Alta Loma Road ☎ 310/657 1333

Wyndham Bel Age ($$$)
All-suite hotel in the heart of West Hollywood. Roof-top swimming pool with fantastic views of the city.
✉ 1020 N San Vicente Boulevard ☎ 310/854 1111

Convenient Location
In Los Angeles, the Westside hotels (from Hollywood to Santa Monica) are probably the best locations for those who wish to visit LA's attractions and enjoy the sights. For the best rates, inquire at the specific hotels for package deals, or call one of the many "brokers" that are emerging in the hotel industry (check local listings for names and numbers).

San Diego/Rest of California

Beside the Sea
The San Diego area is a great place to book into a beachside hotel or resort. The pleasing year-round climate will make it almost irresistible to spend an afternoon by the pool or at the beach. La Jolla, Del Mar and Laguna Beach are just a few areas to look into for a time of rest and relaxation in the sun. Even though winter temperatures are still nearly perfect, many hotels and inns reduce their rates.

San Diego

Bay Club Hotel ($$$)
Large rooms, some with private balconies and patios. Situated on the Marina.
2131 Shelter Island Drive
619/224 8888

Comfort Inn Gaslamp ($$)
In the historic Gaslamp Quarter, and close to the zoo and Balboa Park.
660 G Street **619/238 4100**

Coronado Marriott ($$$)
French and Californian décor on 16 acres (6ha) of exotic landscaped grounds.
2000 Second Street
619/435 3000

Hilton San Diego ($$)
This hotel offers affordable rates near the airport.
1960 Harbor Island Drive
619/291 6700

Horton Grand ($$$)
The oldest building in San Diego (1886). The Horton Grand has Victorian décor with an impressive lobby.
311 Island Avenue
619/544 1886

Hotel del Coronado ($$$)
Famous Victorian hotel jutting out into the bay. Large rooms, some suites. One room is "haunted."
1500 Orange Avenue
619/435 6611

Humphrey's Half Moon Inn ($$)
Beautiful gardens and island décor overlooking the bay.
2303 Shelter Island Drive
619/224 3411

La Costa Resort and Spa ($$$)
Large, luxury resort with golf, tennis and watersports.
2100 Costa Del Mar Road, Carlsbad **760/438 9111**

The Lodge at Torrey Pines ($$$)
Luxurious five-star accomodations in La Jolla. Overlooks the ocean, craftsman-style architecture.
11480 North Torrey Pines Road **858/453 4420**

The Rest of California

Big Bear Lake

Apples Bed & Breakfast Inn ($$)
A secluded setting close to shops and recreation. Afternoon cider and appertizers.
42439 Moonridge Road
909/866 0903

Big Sur

Ventana Inn ($$$)
Luxurious hideaway, comprises 59 separate bungalows. Sweeping views of the coastline.
California Highway 1
831/667 2331

Carmel

Sandpiper Inn ($$)
Early California inn built in 1929. Some rooms with ocean views.
2408 Bay View Avenue
831/624 6433

Tickle Pink Inn at Carmel Highlands ($$$)
Coastline views from secluded cottages and rooms. Nonchalant luxury. Afternoon wine and cheese service.
155 Highland Drive
831/624 1244

Catalina Island

Hotel Metropole ($$$)
Magnificent ocean views from the rooftop sun deck and spa. In Metropole Marketplace.
205 Crescent Avenue, Avalon 310/510 1884

Hotel Vista Del Mar ($$)
Resort hotel overlooking beach with larger, comfortable rooms; most with spectacular views.
417 Crescent Avenue, Avalon 310/510 1452

Death Valley

Furnace Creek Inn ($$$)
Native American décor, built in the 1920s. Choose between regular motel-style rooms and furnished cabins.
About 1 mile (1.6km) south on CA 190 760/786 2345
Oct–May only

Eureka

Best Western Humboldt Bay Inn ($)
Recently remodeled lodging near Humboldt State Park.
232 W 5th Street
707/443 2234

Half Moon Bay

The Beach House ($$$)
Large rooms with ocean views, fireplaces like an old New England summer home. Jacuzzis, saunas.
6 miles (10km) north of Half Moon Bay, 4100 Coast Highway 1 650/712 0220

Lake Arrowhead

Lake Arrowhead Resort ($$)
On the lake in Arrowhead Village. All rooms face the lakefront. Fishing, boating, children's activities.
27984 Highway 189
909/336 1511

Lake Tahoe

Best Western Station House Inn ($$)
Central to the lake, with great sporting activities. Close to the border casinos.
901 Park Avenue, South Lake Tahoe 530/542 1101

Mammoth Lakes

Mammoth Mountain Inn ($$$)
Resort complex; free transportation to the ski areas. Horseback riding and hiking/hunting trails are on offer.
1 Minaret Road 760/934 2581

Mendocino

Headlands Inn ($$)
Remodeled 1868 Victorian with six rooms and one private cottage.
Howard and Albion streets
707/937 4431

Monterey

Old Monterey Inn ($$$)
English country hotel boasting acres of gardens and spectacular views of Monterey Bay.
500 Martin Street
831/375 8284

Morro Bay

Best Western El Rancho ($)
Unique redwood lobby. Very reasonable rates.
2460 Main Street
800/628 3500

Mount Shasta

Tree House Best Western ($$)
Terrific views of the

Bed-and-Breakfast
A recent trend in lodging is the popularity of the bed-and-breakfast and the country inn. Many of these are found in Northern California and Wine Country regions. Many of those who live in the major cities look forward to a weekend in the country at one of these small inns (usually only 10 to 20 rooms). Reservations are difficult to get on the weekends and in the summer, so reserve well in advance.

Motels
For those on a tight budget, it's possible to find a decent motel room (double occupancy) for under $50. Most offer in-room phones, cable television and a pool. There are many motel "chains" that offer safe, clean, reasonably priced lodging for those in transit. Some to look for are Motel 6, Econolodge and Quality Inn.

mountain and excellent skiing in the winter.
✉ **Lake Street just off the I–5**
☎ **530/926 3101**

Ojai

♦♦♦♦Ojai Valley Inn ($$$)
Plush rural surroundings. 220 acres (89ha) that include a championship golf course.
✉ **905 Country Club Road**
☎ **805/646 5511**

Orange County

♦♦♦♦♦Four Seasons Hotel ($$$)
One of the finest hotels in the state. Modern design with tree-lined swimming pool and tennis courts.
✉ **690 Newport Center Drive, Newport Beach** ☎ **949/759 0808**

♦♦♦♦Hilton Waterfront Beach Resort ($$$)
Large resort with beach access, watersports, dining and shopping. Ocean views.
✉ **21100 Pacific Coast Highway, Huntington Beach**
☎ **714/845 8000**

♦♦Hotel Laguna ($$)
Affordable and funky, with private beach for guests.
✉ **425 S Coast Highway, Laguna Beach** ☎ **949/494 1151**

♦♦♦♦Surf and Sand Hotel ($$)
Tasteful, elegant hotel on the beach, near the galleries, shops and restaurants. All rooms with ocean views.
✉ **1555 S Coast Highway, Laguna Beach** ☎ **949/497 4477**

Palm Springs

♦♦The Inn at Deep Canyon ($–$$)
Basic accommodations in Palm Desert; some rooms have kitchenettes.
✉ **74–470 Abronia Trail**
☎ **760/346 8061**

♦♦♦La Mancha Private Villas ($$–$$$)
Two or three bedroomed suites, pools, spas,tennis.
✉ **400 N Avenida Caballeros**
☎ **760/320 0398**

♦♦♦♦Marriott's Desert Springs Resort and Spa ($$$)
Marriott's landmark hotel features an atrium lobby, landscaped gardens, Bob Hope Cultural Center, golf, tennis, man-made beach and an exclusive mall.
✉ **74855 Country Club Drive, Palm Desert** ☎ **760/341 2211**

Two Bunch Palms Inn ($$$)
Secluded cottages on 300 acres. Natural hot springs, a lake and wooded paths.
✉ **67425 Two Bunch Palms Trail, Desert Hot Springs**
☎ **760/329 8791**

Pebble Beach

♦♦♦♦The Lodge at Pebble Beach ($$$)
The epitome of opulence. Overlooks Carmel Bay and the world-famous Pebble Beach golf course.
✉ **1700 17-mile Drive, 3 miles (5km) north of Carmel**
☎ **831/647 7500**

Pismo Beach

♦♦Sea Gypsy Motel ($)
Affordable lodging on the beach.
✉ **1020 Cypress** ☎ **805/773 1801**

Redwood Forest

♦♦♦♦Benbow Inn ($$$)
Mansion built in 1926.

445 Lake Benbow Drive, Garberville 707/923 2124
Closed Jan–Mar

Sacramento

Hyatt Regency ($$)
Located downtown, near the Capitol Building.
1209 "L" Street 916/443 1234

San Luis Obispo

Apple Farm Inn ($$)
A quaint inn complete with working millhouse and bakery.
2015 Monterey Street
805/544 2040

Santa Barbara

Montecito Inn ($$$)
This inn was built in 1928 by Charlie Chaplin and Fatty Arbuckle; the inn takes its facilities and service quite seriously.
1295 Coast Village Road
805/969 7854

Santa Cruz

Sea and Sand Inn ($$)
Budget hotel, overlooking the cliffs.
201 W Cliff Drive
831/427 3400

Solvang

Solvang Royal Scandinavian Inn ($$)
Decorated attractively in Scandinavian style. Centrally located for Solvang's attractions.
400 Alisal Road 805/688 8000

Storybook Inn ($$)
European-style inn offers a retreat-like ambience in the center of town.
409 First Street 805/688 1703

Wine Country

Foothill House ($$$)
Charmingly remodeled, turn-of-the-century farmhouse.
3037 Foothill Boulevard, Calistoga 707/942 6933

Harvest Inn ($$$)
Small English Tudor inn surrounded by vineyards. Many rooms have fireplaces and antique furnishings.
One Main Street, St. Helena
707/963 9463

Napa Inn ($$)
Romantic, turn-of-the-century Queen Anne Victorian. In downtown Napa near shops and restaurants.
1137 Warren Street, Napa
707/257 1444

Silverado Resort ($$$)
Large resort with wine tastings and sport facilities.
1600 Atlas Peak Road, Napa
707/257 0200

Sonoma Mission Inn and Spa ($$$)
Exclusive spa in the Spanish-mission style.
Sonoma Highway, Sonoma
707/938 9000

Trojan Horse Inn ($$)
Only six rooms in this restored frontier home.
19455 Sonoma Highway, Sonoma 707/996 2430

Yosemite

Tenaya Lodge at Yosemite ($$)
Rustic riverside elegance, cookouts and wagon rides.
2 miles (3.2km) south of the park's south gate 559/683 6555

Campgrounds

An alternative to hotels and motels are the state's many campgrounds. Most of the state and national parks have campgrounds that offer tent or RV sites, outdoor cooking areas, public rest rooms and shower facilities. The fee is usually under $10 per night. Private campgrounds adjacent to the parks offer additional facilities at a slightly higher rate. June through September is a busy time.

Art & Antiques/ Fashion/Crafts/Stores

Popular Shopping Venues
San Francisco and Los Angeles are the two most popular shopping areas in California. From large, multi-level shopping centers to streets filled with discount and specialty shops, you can find just about anything your heart desires. Included here are just a few of the most popular areas to get you started. Check the local newspapers, especially on Sunday, for sales and discounts.

Art & Antiques

San Francisco

Fillmore Street
Specialty shops include book and music stores, and clothing from retro to new fashion.
✉ **Jackson & Sutter**

The Japan Center
Art galleries and Oriental gift shops, interspersed with sushi bars and tea houses.
✉ **Bounded by Laguna, Geary, Fillmore, Sutter and Post streets**

Los Angeles

La Cienega Boulevard south of Santa Monica Boulevard, Beverly Boulevard west of the Beverly Center, Melrose Avenue in Hollywood, and Santa Monica's Third Street Promenade are all lined with excellent, but costly antiques stores and art galleries.

San Diego

Antique Row
More than 20 dealers give this street its name.
✉ **Adams Avenue, Kensington**

The Olde Cracker Factory
Antiques center of the area.
✉ **448 W Market** ☎ **619/233 1669**

Rest Of California

Mendocino

This small town in northern California is considered the artistic center of the North Coast.

Mendocino Arts Center
Two art galleries, along with numerous arts and crafts fairs.
✉ **45200 Little Lake Street** ☎ **707/937 5818 and 800/653 3328**

Santa Rosa (Wine Country)

Railroad Square
A historic square featuring antiques stores, curio shops.
☎ **707/578 8478**

Fashion

San Francisco

Haight Street
Famous for hippies in the 1960s; some shops still sell offbeat, vintage clothes. Book and music shops.
✉ **At Ashbury Street**

SoMa
Popular for bargain stores, night-spots and cafés.
✉ **South of Market Street**

Union Square
Large department stores are Macy's, Neiman-Marcus and Saks Fifth Avenue.
✉ **Downtown** ☎ **Macy's 415/397 3333; Neiman-Marcus 415/362 3900; Saks Fifth Avenue 415/986 4300**

Union Street
One of the best streets in San Francisco, with specialist shops/galleries.
✉ **Between Gough and Steiner**

Los Angeles

Garment District
Fashion bargains in open store fronts and inside the huge Cooper Building. Stroll through the California Mart to see upcoming fashions.
✉ **Los Angeles Street and 7th Street, Downtown**

Melrose Avenue
Three-mile (5km) strip of shops from Aardvark's used clothing, to vintage stores and upscale boutiques.
✉ **Between Highland and Doheny, Hollywood**

Rodeo Drive
Renowned as being the most exclusive and expensive shopping area on the West Coast. Top designer clothes and accessories.
✉ **Between Santa Monica and Wilshire boulevards, Beverly Hills**

Venice Beach
Unique and amazingly inexpensive sunwear and hip formal dress.
✉ **Oceanfront Walk, Venice**

San Diego
The Paladion
Posh center with Cartier, Tiffany's, Gucci and more.
✉ **Across from Horton Plaza**

Rest of California

Palm Springs
El Paseo
Exclusive shops that rival Beverly Hills Rodeo Drive. Art galleries.
✉ **Visitors Center, 2901 N Palm Canyon Drive** ☎ **760/778 8418**

Crafts

San Francisco
Fisherman's Wharf
There are four shopping centers here—Pier 39, The Cannery, Ghirardelli Square and The Anchorage.
✉ **Columbus on the Bay**

Los Angeles
Olvera Street
Mexican crafts and gifts, clothing and cafés on LA's oldest street.
✉ **Los Angeles Street**

San Diego
Gaslamp Quarter
A must for the arts and crafts crowd. The Quarter takes in 38 acres (15ha) in the National Historic District.
✉ **Fifth Avenue from Broadway to the waterfront**

Stores

San Francisco
The Embarcadero Center
Shops, restaurants, offices, hotels in a huge downtown complex.
✉ **Sacramento and Clay streets** 🚇 **BART, Muni**

Ghirardelli Square
Formerly a chocolate factory, this area has become a chic center of stores and top restaurants.
✉ **At Fisherman's Wharf**

Los Angeles
Beverly Center
Three-tiered upscale mall, with exterior elevators that offer a great view of the area. Macy's, Broadway, Bullocks, Hard Rock Café.
✉ **Beverly Boulevard and La Cienega, Beverly Hills**

Century City
Features international food court with indoor/outdoor dining, theater, fine dining, Bloomingdale's. Macey's.
✉ **10250 Santa Monica Boulevard, Beverly Hills**

Westside Pavilion
Multi-level with modern, open-air atrium; Nordstrom, Robinsons-May and others.
✉ **Pico and Westwood boulevards**

San Diego
Fashion Valley Mall
This and Mission Valley are the city's two main shopping centres. Six major department stores.
✉ **352 Fashion Valley Road**

Tijuana
Shoppers in San Diego often find themselves drawn to Tijuana, just across the California–Mexico border. The Free-Port status makes for great bargains. Prices are reasonable, and haggling is welcomed as part of the fun. The best shopping areas are the mall at Agua Caliente Race Track and the Avenida Revolución, the city's oldest tourist shopping area. Take precautions with your valuables when traveling across the border.

Factory Outlets/ Produce/Gifts

Outlet and Factory Stores
The latest US shopping trend is outlet and factory stores. Don't be fooled by these "malls," however, as many of the shops rival the parent stores in pricing. Although you have to look carefully, there are enough bargains on the name-brand items to warrant the outlets' popularity. Along the same lines are huge indoor and outdoor flea markets and "swap meets" that offer both new and used items.

Rest of California

Monterey
Cannery Row
Unique shops and restaurants line this nautical area, made famous by John Steinbeck's novel *Cannery Row.*
✉ **Fisherman's Wharf**

Orange County
South Coast Plaza
This is Orange County's largest and most exclusive mall, with three huge sections connected by free tram. All major department stores are located within this complex, along with a wide variety of specialty stores.

Factory Outlets

Folsom
Folsom Factory Store
The 50 stores here include names like Nike, Jones NY, Bass.
✉ **13000 Folsom**

Gilroy
Outlets at Gilroy
More than 100 stores. Includes Gap, Ann Taylor, Espirit among others.
✉ **681 Leavesley**

Lake Elsinore
Lake Elsinore Outlet Center
Van Huesen and Levi's are just two of the 70 stores located here.
✉ **17600 Collier Avenue**

Mammoth Lakes
Mammoth Factory Store
Only 10 stores, but they are some of the best, with names like Ralph Lauren, and Bass.
✉ **3343 Main Street**

Monterey
American Tin Cannery Factory Outlet
Izod and Nine West are just two of the nearly 40 stores.
✉ **125 Ocean View Boulevard, Pacific Grove**

Petaluma
Petaluma Village Factory Outlet
Fifty stores from Saks to Coach to Gap.
✉ **2200 Petaluma Boulevard**

Pismo Beach
Pismo Beach Outlet Center
Jones New York, Bass, Mikasa, Levi's; 40 shops in all.
✉ **333 5-Cities Drive**

Solvang
Solvang Outlet Stores
Small but élite, featuring Donna Karen, Ellen Tracy, Brooks Bros.
✉ **3202 N Alisal Road**

Wine Country
Napa Factory Store
Liz Claiborne, J. Crew, Tommy Hilfiger; 50 in all.
✉ **629 Factory Street Drive, Napa**

Produce

San Francisco
Chinatown
Almost as fun as finding unique produce and great bargains is watching the locals wrangle for better prices.
✉ **Bordered by Broadway, Bush, Kearny and Powell streets**

Los Angeles
Farmers Market
Over 100 sellers of not only fresh produce but gifts, food and clothes, all at affordable

prices. Open-air cafés (➤ 49).
✉ **Third and Fairfax, Hollywood**

Gifts

San Francisco

Chinatown
Asian specialty shops, fresh produce, and incredible architecture (➤ 35).
✉ **Bordered by Broadway, Bush, Kearny & Powell streets**

Fisherman's Wharf
Street performers entertain as you explore the 100 shops and restaurants clustered around the piers (➤ 36).
✉ **Between The Embarcadero and Columbus Avenue**

Los Angeles

Hollywood Boulevard
The place to go to find rare movie memorabilia and posters. Theaters and restaurants for every mood and budget.
✉ **Between La Brea and Highland**

Little Tokyo
Unusual Oriental items. Outdoor shopping/dining.
✉ **San Pedro & First streets, Downtown**

Venice Beach
Outdoor booths with great prices, if you aren't distracted by the street artists and Muscle Beach iron-pumpers.
✉ **Oceanfront between Washington & Santa Monica Boulevards**

San Diego

Old Town
Small gift boutiques and cafés among flower gardens, fountains and courtyards in the style of a Mexican marketplace. One of the best antiques shopping areas in Southern California. Bargain prices for valuable items at local antiques shops.
✉ **Mason Street and San Diego Avenue**

Rest of California

Monterey Bay

Peter Rabbit and Friends
Toys, music boxes and clothing featuring some of the characters and scenes from Beatrix Potter's children's stories.
✉ **Lincoln Avenue between 7th and Ocean avenues**
☎ **831/624 6854**

Sacramento

David Berkeley's
Eclectic variations from extensive wine selections by White House wine consultant, David Berkeley, to Epicurean European foods and country-flavored gifts.
✉ **515 Pavillions Lane**
☎ **916/929 4422**

Wine Country

All Seasons Cafe Wine Shop
A selection of the best of the hundreds of wine shops in Napa Valley. Most sell gifts and other unique products, and will ship anywhere in the world.
✉ **1400 Lincoln Avenue, Calistoga** ☎ **707/942 9111**

Shaker Shops West
Quality reproductions of Shaker furniture and gifts, deep in California's north country.
✉ **5 Inverness Way, Inverness**
☎ **415/669 7256**

Farmers' Markets
Almost every city and town in California has an open-air or farmers' market, and roadside stands dot country roads and state highways. These markets are great places to find unique gifts or cherished mementoes of your visit, and their prices are generally lower than more urban retailers. Whatever type of shopping you prefer, locals residents are happy to point you to the most popular shopping places.

Children's Attractions

Avoid the Long Lines
Most of the larger California cities have fine museums that are inexpensive and provide interactive exhibits. A hint for avoiding long lines at theme parks is to arrive early, or just an hour or two before closing.

San Francisco

Children's Fairyland
This inexpensive 10-acre (4-ha) park, with exhibits from nursery rhymes, is said to have intrigued Walt Disney so much he built Disneyland Park to copy it.
699 Bellevue Avenue 510/238 6876 Fri–Sun 10–4; extended hours in summer

Paramount's Great America
The Bay area's place for roller coasters and other daredevil rides. Fort-Fun is an interactive parent/child area. Top Gun and Smurf Woods rides are the most popular. Also features stage shows, musicals, puppet shows and wildlife shows.
Great American Parkway, Santa Clara (about 45 miles/73km south of San Francisco) 408/988 1776 Sat, Sun 10–7; weekdays summer only

Raging Waters
The Bay area's only water theme park, with large and long waterslides designed to please. There are over 30 different attractions. Older children will love the innertube rides.
Lake Cunningham Park, San Jose 408/238 9900 May–Sep, call for hours

Santa Cruz Beach Boardwalk
This historical landmark, dating to 1907, was the first full-scale amusement park on the West Coast. With roller-coasters and haunted castles, bumper cars and a ferris wheel, this is an "oldie but goodie."
400 Beach Street, Santa Cruz 831/423 5590 Call for hours

Los Angeles

Disneyland Park (► 18)

Hollywood Guinness World of Records
Trivia galore from The-Animal-with-The-Smallest-Brain-in-Proportion-to-Body-Size (a Stegosaurus) to The Most Biographed Female (Marilyn Monroe).
6764 Hollywood Boulevard, Hollywood 323/463 6433 Daily 10am–11pm Moderate

Hollywood Wax Museum (► 51)

Knott's Berry Farm (► 78)

The Pacific Ocean
The whole family can frolic on one of the many beaches that line the Pacific Ocean. Venice offers bicycle, skateboard and stroller rentals and playgrounds; the Pier at Santa Monica has rides, including the indoor carousel seen in the movie *The Sting*, arcades and shops; Malibu Beach is home to many celebrities. Further north on Pacific Coast Highway are more sandy beaches for sunning, swimming and surfing (like Leo Carillo, Zuma, Monterey Presidio), and there are even campgrounds right on the beach for a minimum cost. Summer reservations a must.

Universal Studios (► 54)

San Diego

Balboa Park (► 16)

Legoland California
This Danish import opened in 1999, and the entire park is built out of lego pieces.

Rides and exhibits are usually packed.
✉ 1 Lego Drive, Carlsbad ☎ 760/918 5346 ⌚ Call for hours 💰 Expensive

San Diego Zoo (► 16)
☎ 619/234 3153 ⌚ Daily 9–4; zoo grounds close at 6pm 💰 Inexpensive

Sea World (► 64)

Rest of California

La Habra

Children's Museum at La Habra
Restored railroad station exhibiting a wide range of scientific and historical artifacts. Special events and programs.
✉ 301 Euclid Street, La Habra ☎ 562/905 9793 ⌚ Mon 10–1, Tue–Sat 10–5, Sun 1–5 💰 Inexpensive

Lake Arrowhead

Lake Arrowhead Children's Museum
Contains historical information on the area and anthropological exhibitions. Kids can pretend they are ants in a life-size colony.
✉ Lake Arrowhead Village ☎ 909/336 3093 ⌚ Daily 10–5, 10–6 in summer 💰 Inexpensive

Paso Robles

Atascadero Lake Park and Charles Paddock Zoo
Intimate zoo with jaguars from Brazil, Bengal tigers, pink flamingos and lots of chimps. Nominal entry fee. Next to the zoo is a beautiful lake with picnic facilities.
✉ State Route 41, south of Paso Robles ☎ 805/461 5080 ⌚ Zoo: daily 10–4, 10–5 in summer. Lake Park: daily until sundown

Lake Nacimiento Resort
One of the most popular family resorts in the state. Great outdoor activities, including fishing and diving. Features a full-service marina and dock where you can rent anything from jet-skis to pontoon boats. Lodge, campgrounds and RV facilities.
✉ County Road G–14 out of Paso Robles ☎ 805/238 3256 ⌚ Daily to sundown

Sacramento

Six Flags Waterworld
This park has some of the best high-speed slides and other water attractions.
✉ Exposition Boulevard ☎ 916/924 0556 ⌚ Late May–early Sep; call for hours 💰 Expensive

Santa Ana

Kidseum
Kids won't even realize they're being educated about world cultures as they take part in the storytelling, puppet shows and other exhibits at this interactive museum.
✉ 1802 Main Street ☎ 714/567 3600 (Bowes Museum and College of Art) ⌚ Summer Tue–Sun noon–4; winter Sat–Sun 11–4

Valencia

Six Flags Magic Mountain
Specializing in thrill rides, the park also offers a mini-zoo and the Wizard's Village for the younger members of the family. Admission price covers everything but food, including puppet shows, dance revues and other live entertainment.
✉ 26101 Magic Mountain Parkway, off Interstate 5 Freeway ☎ 661/255 4103 ⌚ Call for hours

Pacifying the Kids
For enjoyable travel with children, don't overdo it. Adult stress reflects in youngsters. Kids love to help plan excursions and navigate from the map, and allowing them to do so teaches valuable skills. To avoid grouchy kids and frazzled adults, take frequent breaks, especially on long road trips. And most importantly, see the sights through their eyes for a unique perspective often lost in the grown-up world.

Museums/Concert Halls/Nightlife

TV and Film
California's film industry means major cities teem with movie theaters. Check local papers for listings or pick up a free *LA* or *San Francisco Weekly* at restaurants, shops. For variation, there's the Silent Movie theater (Hollywood), the alternative Red Vic Movie House (Haight), the live vaudevillian Fabulous Palm Springs Follies (☎ 760/327 0225), or join a television studio audience (☎ 818/506 0043).

Museums

San Francisco

Exploratorium/Palace of Fine Arts
Crème de la crème of science museums. Exhibits of art, science and human perception. The Tactile Dome is wonderful.
✉ 3601 Lyon Street ☎ 415/561 0360 🕔 Tue–Sun 10–5, Mon, hols 10–5, Memorial Day–Labor Day daily 10–6

SFMOMA (► 39)
✉ 151 Third Street ☎ 415/357 4000 🕔 Mon, Tue, Fri–Sun 11–5.45, Thu 11–8.45; closed Wed 💲 Free 1st Tue of month

Los Angeles

Armand Hammer Museum of Art and Cultural Center
Holds the largest US collection of French artist Honoré Dumier.
✉ 10899 Wilshire Westwood ☎ 310/443 7000 🕔 Tue, Wed, Fri, Sat 11–7, Thu 11–9, Sun 11–5

California Museum of Science & Industry (► 50)
✉ 700 State Drive, Exposition Park ☎ 323/724 3623 🕔 Daily 10–5

Huntington Library, Art Gallery and Botanical Gardens (► 52)
✉ 1151 Oxford Road, San Marino ☎ 626/405 2141

Museum of Contemporary Art (MOCA) (► 53)
✉ 250 S Grand Avenue ☎ 213/626 6222

Museum of Tolerance
Interactive exhibits of hate activities (Holocaust, riots) designed to promote understanding.
✉ 9786 W Pico ☎ 310/553 8403 🕔 Mon–Thu 11.30–4, Fri 11.30–3 (1pm Nov–Mar), Sun 11–5 💲 Moderate

Rest of California

Monterey

Pacific House
Old West hotel and saloon-turned-museum.
✉ 10 Custom House Plaza ☎ 831/649 7118 🕔 Tue–Sun 10–4

Sacramento

Crocker Art Museum
Oldest art museum in the American West. European, Asian and California art in 19th-century building.
✉ 216 "O" Street ☎ 916/264 5423 🕔 Tue–Sun 10–5, Thu 10–9

Concert Halls

San Francisco

Louise M. Davies Symphony Hall
Symphonies, concerts; also tours of this stream-lined glass-and-granite building.
✉ Van Ness Avenue and Grove Street, Civic Center ☎ 415/864 6000

Los Angeles

Hollywood Bowl
Outdoor arena, year-round headline concerts of every music style, especially the LA Philharmonic.
✉ 2301 N Highland Avenue, Hollywood ☎ 323/850 2000

Wiltern Theatre
Intimate, acoustically wonderful hall that features top-name musical performances in the art deco Wiltern Center.
✉ Wilshire and Western ☎ 213/480 3232

San Diego
Civic Theatre
Ultramodern design provides a great backdrop to concerts held here.
✉ San Diego Concourse, 202 "C" Street ☎ 619/615 4100

Nightlife

San Francisco

Bottom of the Hill
Alternative bands head to this Potrero Hill club, which has a beer garden, pool tables and also serves food.
✉ 1233 17th Street
☎ 415/621 4455 (information line)

111 Minna
An art gallery that does double duty as a DJ/dance venue in the evenings.
✉ 111 Minna Street, at 2nd Street ☎ 415/974 1719

Vesuvio Cafe
This former haunt of Beat poets hasn't changed much in 30 years.
✉ 255 Columbus Avenue
☎ 415/362 3370

Los Angeles

The Baked Potato
Oldest major contemporary jazz club in California. Big-name entertainment for a moderate cost.
✉ 3787 Cahuenga Boulevard W, North Hollywood
☎ 818/980 1615

Bar Marmont
Intimate French colonial café, usually full of celebrities and paparazzi.
✉ 6171 Sunset Boulevard, Hollywood ☎ 323/650 0575

BB King's Blues Club
Three floors. Lucille's room is acoustic on Fri and Sat.
✉ 1000 Universal City Drive, Universal City ☎ 818/622 5464

Cat & Fiddle Pub and Restaurant
Ambient outdoor patio. Sunday jazz jam. No cover.
✉ 6530 Sunset Boulevard, Hollywood ☎ 323/468 3800

Cowboy Palace Saloon
The last real honky tonk in California. Live country seven nights. Pool, darts, dance classes. No cover.
✉ 21635 Devonshire Street, Chatsworth ☎ 818/341 0166

Good Luck Bar
Knocked out of the No. 1 spot by Bar Marmont, but now you finally have room to dance and enjoy yourself.
✉ 1514 Hillhurst Avenue, Los Feliz ☎ 323/666 3524

The Improvisation (Improv)
See the place where many comedians got their start.
✉ 8162 Melrose, West Hollywood ☎ 323/651 2583

Molly Malone's Irish Pub
Small neighborhood bar with Irish folk, rock & roll, R & B nightly. Cover varies.
✉ 575 S Fairfax ☎ 323/935 1577

Rage
Gay/lesbian meeting place, alternative/underground music.
✉ 8911 Santa Monica Boulevard, West Hollywood
☎ 310/652 7055

San Diego

Top O' the Cove
Piano bar/restaurant featuring show tunes and standards.
✉ 1216 Prospect Street, La Jolla ☎ 858/454 7779

Out on the Town
Karaoke's hot, but there's no lack of other choices for night-time entertainment in California: headline concerts to acoustical folk by local solo artists, poetry-readings to comedy, dramatic plays and musicals to raunchy revues. Even in the small communities, you can find live entertainment, with country music being the most popular. Parking can be difficult in Los Angeles, but valet parking is available at a reasonable cost.

Nightlife/Performing Arts Theaters/Sports

Pro Sports
For those who would rather watch than participate, pro sports are abundant in the state. Besides pro golf tours, there are several renowned horse-racing parks, especially Del Mar, a beachside track just north of San Diego. San Diego has pro baseball and football; LA has Clippers and Lakers basketball, baseball and hockey; San Diego has baseball, football, soccer and ice hockey. The Bay Area has pro baseball, football, basketball and hockey. Information can be obtained from team offices. College sports add elan to the mix.

Nightlife

Rest of California

Eureka

Lost Coast Brewery & Café
Microbreweries are the rage, and this is one of the best.
617 Fourth Street
707/445 4480

Sacramento

Harlow's
Most glamorous nightclub in town. Upstairs is Momo's cigar lounge.
2708 "J" Street **916/441 4693**

The Monkey Bar
Favorite haunt of the hip. Arrive early if you want to sit.
2730 Capitol Avenue
916/442 8490

Sacramento Brewing Company's Oasis
Locally produced, award-winning beer.
7811 Capitol Avenue
916/966 6274

Performing Arts/ Theaters

San Francisco

Orpheum Theatre
The largest touring shows to San Francisco play here.
1192 Market Street
415/551 2000

American Conservatory Theater (ACT)
One of the top regional theaters in the US.
415 Geary Street
415/749 2228

Los Angeles

Music Center of Los Angeles County
Includes Dorothy Chandler Pavilion, Mark Taper Forum, featuring experiment plays; the Ahmanson, with musical comedies and the Walt Disney Concert Hall.
135 N Grand, downtown
213/972 7211

San Diego

Lawrence Welk Resort Theatre
Dinner theater, with Broadway and Broadway-style shows. Buffet matinee and evening.
8860 Lawrence Welk Drive, Escondido **760/749 3448**

Sledgehammer Theatre
Avant-garde productions.
1620 Sixth Avenue
619/544 1484

Rest of California

Orange County

Orange County Performing Arts Center
Regular performances by New York City Opera, American Ballet Theater and Los Angeles Philharmonic Orchestra, plus present-ations of popular musicals.
600 Town Center Drive, Costa Mesa **714/556 2787**

Spectator Sports

Los Angeles

Los Angeles Galaxy
The Los Angeles soccer team play at the Home Depot Center.
18400 Avalon Boulevard, Carson **310/630 2200**

Indio

Eldorado Polo Club
The "Winter Polo Capital of the West." Weekday practice matches are free. Picnic grounds.
50–950 Madison Street
760/342 2223

Monterey

Mazda Raceway Laguna Seca

Four major auto races a year, including restored antique cars.

1021 Monterey Road, Salinas 93908 831/648 5100

Sports

San Francisco

Several companies along the wharf offer sailing, fishing excursions and boat rentals. Some off-pier fishing as well.

Los Angeles

Moonlight Rollerway

Moonlight is one of the more popular indoor roller-blading rinks in LA.

5110 San Fernando Road, Glendale 818/241 3630

Pershing Square

The outdoor ice rink opens in November.

Pershing Square Station on Metro Red Line 818/243 6488

Santa Anita Race Track

Bet on horses during the track's season, from December to April.

285 West Huntington Drive 626/574 7223 Dec 26–late Apr

Sports Center Bowl

The landmark Jerry's Deli is right next door for a snack, after you've worked up an appetite.

12655 Ventura Boulevard, Studio City 818/769 7600 Call for open bowling hours

Rest of California

Lake Tahoe

Ski Lake Tahoe Association

Package deals available on the 15 downhill and 11 cross-country ski areas. Free shuttle between all.

888/824 6338 (Snow Ski); 530/544 7747 (Water Ski School)

Monterey

Monterey Bay Kayaks

Kayak rentals, tours.

693 Del Monte Avenue 831/373 5357

Palm Springs

Mission Hills Resort Golf Club

One reason Palm Springs is "Winter Golf Capital of the World."

71–501 Dinah Shore Drive, Rancho Mirage 760/328 3198

Palm Springs Tennis Center

Nine lighted courts open to the public.

1300 Baristo Road 760/320 0020

Pebble Beach

Spyglass Hill

Less expensive than Pebble Beach course (which hosts the AT&T ProAm tour), the bordering Pacific and Del Monte Forest make this difficult but scenic. Reserve a month in advance (year for groups).

Spyglass Hill Road 831/624 3811

Solvang

Windhaven Glider

Breathtaking glider rides.

Santa Ynez Airport 805/688 2517 10–5 daily

Yosemite

Try rock-climbing, backpacking, camping, and hiking, guided or not. Sheer El Capitan mountain, at 3,500ft (1067m), attracts world-class climbers in search of a challenge.

Choices

California offers the unique opportunity to visit multiple environments, all within a 24-hour period. You can spend the morning backpacking in the desert, the afternoon riding horses on wooded mountain trails, then head for the ocean for clam-digging or shell-hunting, and a sail into the sunset. For something different, cruise over to Mexico for some fast-paced jai alai (Fronton Palacio, 619/298 4105).

What's On When

The following are just a few of California's myriad festivals and celebrations.

January
Tournament of Roses Parade, Pasadena
Palm Springs International Film Festival

February
Chinese New Year Celebration, San Francisco
Napa Valley Mustard Celebration, Napa

March
International Asian Film Festival, San Francisco
Los Angeles Marathon
Mendocino Whale Festival

April
Toyota Grand Prix, Long Beach
Cherry Blossom Festival, San Francisco
Palm Desert Springfest, Palm Desert
Cinco De Mayo Celebration, state-wide

May
San Francisco International Film Fest
Muscle Car Show, Bakersfield
Sacramento Jazz Jubilee
San Francisco Bay to Breakers, a race where people run in costume

June
Scottish Highlands Games and Gathering of the Clans, Modesto
Amador County Wine Festival, Plymouth
Sonoma Valley Shakespeare Festival, Sonoma

July
Festival of Arts and Pageant of the Masters, Laguna Beach
California Rodeo, Salinas
Greek Festival, Santa Barbara
San Francisco Marathon

August
Mozart Festival, San Luis Obispo
Sawdust Festival, Laguna Beach
San Francisco Mime Troupe Summer Park Season
Old Spanish Days Fiesta, Santa Barbara
Japanese Cultural Bazaar, Sacramento
California State Fair, Sacramento
Children's Festival of the Arts, Hollywood

September
Greek Food Festival, Sacramento
Oktoberfest, Huntington Beach
Danish Days, Solvang
Monterey Jazz Festival, Monterey
Armenian Food Festival, San Francisco
Bowlful of Blues Festival, Ojai
California International Air Show, Salinas

October
Jazz Festival, San Francisco
Rose Show, Santa Barbara
San Francisco Fleet week

November
West Coast Ragtime Festival, in various locations
Christmas Parade, Hollywood

December
America's Tallest Living Christmas Tree, Ferndale
Newport Harbor Christmas Boat Parade, Newport Beach
Celebrity Cooks and Kitchens Tour, Mendocino

Practical Matters

Above: *T-shirts at Venice Beach*
Right: *Having fun on the Boardwalk at Santa Cruz, a traditional American seaside resort*

TIME DIFFERENCES

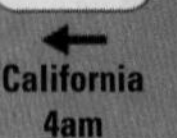

GMT	California	Germany	USA (NY)	Netherlands	Spain
12 noon	4am	1pm	7am	1pm	1pm

BEFORE YOU GO

WHAT YOU NEED

● Required
○ Suggested
▲ Not required

Some countries require a passport to remain valid for a minimum period (usually at least six months) beyond the date of entry—contact their consulate

	UK	Germany	USA	Netherlands	Spain
Passport	●	●	▲	●	●
Visa (regulations can change—check before booking your trip)	▲	▲	▲	▲	▲
Onward or Return Ticket	●	●	▲	●	●
Health Inoculations	▲	▲	▲	▲	▲
Health Documentation (➤ 123, Health)	●	●	●	●	●
Travel Insurance	○	○	○	○	○
Driving Licence (national)	●	●	●	●	●
Car Insurance Certificate (if own car)	○	○	○	○	○

WHEN TO GO

San Francisco

High season

Low season

JAN	FEB	MAR	APR	MAY	JUN	JUL	AUG	SEP	OCT	NOV	DEC
13°C	14°C	17°C	18°C	19°C	21°C	22°C	22°C	23°C	22°C	18°C	14°C

Very wet Wet Cloud Sun

TOURIST OFFICES

In the UK
Visit USA Association
☎ 09069 101020
(consumer line)
www.visitusa.org.uk

In the USA
California Division of Tourism
801 K Street, Suite 1600,
Sacramento, CA 95812
☎ 916/444 4429,
call-free 800/862 2543;
fax: 916/322 3402
www.visitcalifornia.com

POLICE 911

FIRE 911

AMBULANCE 911

WHEN YOU ARE THERE

ARRIVING

International direct flights operate into Los Angeles (☎ 310/646 5252)—one of the world's busiest airports—and San Francisco (☎ 650/821 8211). San Diego Airport also has international flights but most stop en route first. Charter flights also use these airports.

Los Angeles Airport
Miles to city center

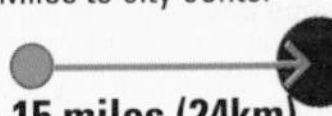

15 miles (24km)

Journey times

 45–60 minutes

 35 minutes

30 minutes

San Francisco Airport
Miles to city center

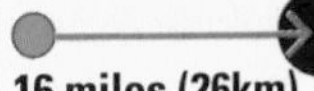

16 miles (26km)

Journey times

 N/A

 30–60 minutes

30 minutes

MONEY

The American monetary unit is the dollar ($), which is divided into 100 cents. There are coins of 1 cent (penny), 5 cents (nickel), 10 cents (dime), 25 cents (quarter), 50 cents (half dollar) and 1 dollar. Notes (bills) are in denominations of 1, 2, 5, 10, 20, 50 and 100 dollars. Be warned, though: all notes, whatever their value, are *exactly the same color (green) and size.*

TIME

California is on Pacific Standard Time; eight hours behind Greenwich Mean Time (GMT-8), but from early April, when clocks are put forward one hour, to late October, Daylight Saving Time (GMT-7) operates. California is also three hours behind the east coast of the USA (Eastern Standard

CUSTOMS

YES

Goods Obtained Duty Free for Import into the USA:
Alcohol (spirits): 1L
Cigarettes: 200 *or*
Cigars (not Cuban): 50 *or*
Tobacco: 4.4 pounds (*or* proportionate amounts of each).
Gifts up to the value of $100 (including 100 cigars in addition to the tobacco allowance above); only for non-US residents and may only be claimed once in six months.
(You must be 21 and over to benefit from the alcohol allowance and over 17 for the tobacco allowance.)

NO

Drugs, firearms, ammunition, offensive weapons, explosives, obscene material, some foods and agricultural items.

CONSULATES

UK
310/481 0031 (LA)

Germany
323/930 2703 (LA)
415 775 1061 (SF)

Netherlands
310 268 1598 (LA)

Spain
323/938 0158 (LA)
415 922 2995 (SF)

WHEN YOU ARE THERE

TOURIST OFFICES

- Anaheim/ Orange County Visitor & Convention Bureau, 800 West Katella Avenue, Anaheim, CA 92802, ☎ 714/765 8857
- California Deserts Tourism Association, 37–115 Palm View Road, Rancho Mirage, CA 92270, ☎ 760/328 9256
- Los Angeles Convention & Visitors Bureau, 685 Figueroa Street, Los Angeles, CA 90017 ☎ 213/689 8822
- Monterey Peninsula Visitors & Convention Bureau, 150 Oliver Street, PO Box 1770, Monterey, CA 93940, ☎ 831/649 1770
- Palm Springs Tourism, 777 N Canyon Drive, Suite 201, Palm Springs, CA 92264, ☎ 760/778 8415
- Sacramento Convention & Visitors Bureau, 1608 I Street, Sacramento, CA 95814, ☎ 916/264 7777
- San Diego Convention & Visitors Bureau, 401 B Street, Suite 1400, San Diego, CA 92101, ☎ 619/236 1212
- San Francisco Convention & Visitors Bureau, 201 Third Street, Suite 900, San Francisco, CA 94103, ☎ 415/974 6900

NATIONAL HOLIDAYS

J	F	M	A	M	J	J	A	S	O	N	D
2	2			1		1		2	1	2	1

Jan 1	New Year's Day
Jan (3rd Mon)	Martin Luther King Jr's Birthday
Feb 12	Lincoln's Birthday
Feb (3rd Mon)	President's Day
Jul 4	Independence Day
Sep (1st Mon)	Labor Day
Oct (2nd Mon)	Columbus Day
Nov 11	Veteran's Day
Nov (4th Thu)	Thanksgiving Day
Dec 25	Christmas Day

On these days shops, banks and businesses close.

OPENING HOURS

○ Shops	● Attractions/museums
● Offices	● Post offices
● Banks	● Pharmacies

9am | 10am | 11am | 12pm | 2pm | 3pm | 4pm | 5pm | 6pm

☐ Day ☐ Midday
☐ Evening

In addition to the times shown above, many shops, particularly department stores within shopping malls, are open evenings and during afternoons on Sunday. Some supermarkets and grocery shops open 24 hours. Banks open until 5.30pm Friday and some major banks open on Saturday. Banks in some major towns and tourist areas may have longer hours. Some pharmacies open from 7am to 9pm or even midnight, while some open 24 hours. Opening times of attractions and museums vary (see individual entries in the What to See section). Some post offices open

PUBLIC TRANSPORT

Internal Flights Flying is the quickest way of getting around California and is not all that expensive if you take advantage of deals offered by airlines. The international airports of San Francisco, Oakland, Los Angeles and San Diego connect with a number of regional airports.

Trains Rail service is provided by America's National Railroad Corporation, Amtrak, which serves 72 California cities and towns. Carriages are clean, comfortable and rarely crowded. A Far Western Region Rail Pass (available only outside the US) gives 45 days unlimited travel over the far Western states.

Long Distance Buses Buses are by far the cheapest way of getting around. Greyhound Lines operates an inter-city service and also links many smaller towns within California. The Ameripass (only available outside the US) gives 4, 5, 7, 15, 30 or 60 days unlimited travel throughout the USA.

Ferries A ferry service links San Francisco with the Bay communities of Sausalito, Larkspur and Tiburon in scenic Marin County, and to Vallejo, Oakland and Alameda (departures from Pier 1, foot of Market Street). There is also a boat service from Long Beach and Newport Beach to Catalina Island.

Urban Transportation Local communities and major cities are served by local bus services. In addition, San Francisco has cable-cars serving the downtown area and the BART train system covering the Bay areas. Los Angeles has its metrorail and San Diego has a trolley car service through the downtown area.

CAR RENTAL

If planning to rent a car, consider the fly/drive programs many airline offer before you go. Other-wise most car rental companies have offices throughout the state. Charges depend on size of car, locale and time of year. Pay by credit card to avoid hefty cash deposit.

CABS

Cabs may be hailed on the street but few cruise outside tourist areas. If you are away from airports or major hotels it is best to phone for one (look under "cabs" in Yellow Pages). In most cities rates are high, except San Francisco because of its comparatively small size.

DRIVING

Speed limits on rural interstate roads (motorways): **70mph/113kph**

Speed limits on many freeways (two-lane or more carriageways): **65mph/105kph**

Speed limits in residential and business districts and school zones: **25mph/ 40kph (or as signposted)**

Must be worn in front seats at all times and in rear seats where fitted.

Random breath-testing. Never drive under the influence of alcohol.

Petrol (gasoline or gas), leaded and unleaded, is sold in US gal (3.8L). Most petrol stations are self service. When removing the nozzle from the pump you must lift or turn the lever to activate it. Petrol is more expensive in remote areas and you may be charged more if paying by credit card.

If you break down in a rented car, phone the emergency number on the dashboard. Summon help from emergency telephones located along freeways (every ½ mile) and remote highways (every 2 miles/ 3km), or sit tight and wait for the cruising highway patrol or state patrol to spot you (a raised bonnet should help).

0 1 2 3 4 5 6 7 8
CENTIMETRES

INCHES
0 1 2 3

PERSONAL SAFETY

California is certainly not crime free and drugs are a problem, but exercise due caution, especially in downtown areas, and you should be safe. Away from these areas crime is quite low key. Some precautions:

- Do not peer at a map at every street corner, suggesting you are a lost tourist.
- If confronted by a mugger, hand over your money.
- If driving do not stop the car in any unlit or deserted urban area.

Police assistance:
☎ 911
from any call box

TELEPHONES

Telephones are located in hotel and motel lobbies, drugstores, restaurants, garages and in roadside kiosks. Exact change in 5, 10 and 25 cent pieces is required to place a call. For internal calls dial 1 before the number when the area code is different from the one on the phone you are using. For the operator dial 0, for directory assistance dial 411.

International Dialling Codes

From the USA to:	
UK:	**011 44**
Germany:	**011 49**
Netherlands:	**011 31**
Spain:	**011 34**

POST

Post Offices
Post offices are plentiful in cities. Stamps are also sold from stamp machines in hotels and shops but have a 25 percent mark up. Main post offices in larger cities normally open 8–6 (noon Sat); closed: Sun. ☎ 213/483 3745 (LA); ☎ 415/487 8981 (San Fran)

ELECTRICITY

The power supply is:
110–115 volts

Round 3-hole sockets taking plugs with 2 flat pins in a parallel position, with an upper, round, earth pin for earthed appliances. European visitors should bring a voltage transformer as well as an adaptor.

TIPS/GRATUITIES

Yes ✓ No ✕		
Restaurants	✓	15–20%
Cafeterias/fast-food outlets	✕	
Bars	✓	15–20%
Cabs	✓	15–20%
Porters	✓	$1/bag
Chambermaids	✓	$1/day
Usherettes	✕	
Hairdressers	✓	10–15%
Cloakroom attendants	✓	$1/coat
Lavatories	✕	

PHOTOGRAPHY

What to photograph: alpine ranges, redwood forests, thundering rivers, crystal-clear lakes, spectacular deserts, sunny beaches, glitzy cities.
Where to buy film: drugstores and supermarkets are probably the cheapest places; you will pay more at specialized kiosks near major tourist attractions.
Video film: the format used for video cassettes in the US differs from that used in the UK. You cannot buy videos in the US compatible with a video camera bought in the UK.

HEALTH

Insurance

There is no agreement for medical treatment between the US and other countries and all travelers MUST be covered by medical insurance (for an unlimited amount of medical costs is advisable). Treatment will be refused without evidence of insurance.

Dental Services

Medical insurance (see above) will cover you for dental treatment. In the event of any emergency, see your hotel concierge or consult the Yellow Pages for an emergency dentist.

Sun Advice

California enjoys a lot of sunshine with more than 250 clear days a year. Along the coast mornings can be hazily overcast and sea breezes (especially in the north) can make it feel cooler than it is. Protect the skin at all times.

Drugs

Quick-remedy medicines such as aspirin are readily available at any pharmacy (drugstore). For tablets containing acetaminophen read paracetamol. Also, many pain-killing pills available "over the counter" at home may need a prescription in the US.

Safe Water

It is quite safe to drink tap water. In hotels and restaurants a nice touch is that water, generally ice cold, is provided free with meals. Bottled water is also widely available but is not as popular as in Europe.

CONCESSIONS

Students Upon production of ID proving student status, there are discounts available on travel, theater and museum tickets, plus at some nightspots. It is always worth asking at the outset.

Senior Citizens For anyone over the age of 62 there is a tremendous variety of discounts on offer (upon proof of age). Both Amtrak (train) and Greyhound (bus), as well as many US airlines, offer (smallish) percentage reductions on fares. Museums, art galleries, attractions, cinemas, and even hotels offer small discounts, and as the definition of senior can drop to as low as 55, it is always worth enquiring.

CLOTHING SIZES

USA	UK	Europe	
36	36	46	Suits
38	38	48	
40	40	50	
42	42	52	
44	44	54	
46	46	56	
8	7	41	Shoes
8.5	7.5	42	
9.5	8.5	43	
10.5	9.5	44	
11.5	10.5	45	
12	11	46	
14.5	14.5	37	Shirts
15	15	38	
15.5	15.5	39/40	
16	16	41	
16.5	16.5	42	
17	17	43	
6	8	34	Dresses
8	10	36	
10	12	38	
12	14	40	
14	16	42	
16	18	44	
6	4.5	38	Shoes
6.5	5	38	
7	5.5	39	
7.5	6	39	
8	6.5	40	
8.5	7	41	

WHEN DEPARTING

- Contact the airport or airline the day prior to leaving to ensure flight details are unchanged.
- Departure tax: all airport, customs and security taxes are included in the price of the ticket.
- Check the duty-free limits of the country you are entering before departure.

LANGUAGE

English is the official language of the USA. Californians, however, are a fascinating mix of cultures, most notably of Spanish or Mexican extraction. In fact, Spanish is heard throughout California. Spanish is met in many forms, for instance in city and street names. The five largest cities in California: Los Angeles, San Diego, San Francisco, San Jose and Sacramento bear Spanish names. However, although English is the native language there are many differences between its British and American usage. Some of the more commonly encountered are listed below:

British	American	British	American
holiday	*vacation*	eiderdown	*comforter*
fortnight	*two weeks*	tap	*faucet*
ground floor	*first floor*	luggage	*baggage*
first floor	*second floor*	hotel porter	*bellhop*
second floor	*third floor*	chambermaid	*room maid*
flat	*apartment*	surname	*last name*
lift	*elevator*	cupboard	*closet*

British	American	British	American
cheque	*check*	25 cent coin	*quarter*
traveller's cheque	*traveler's check*	banknote	*bill*
I cent coin	*penny*	banknote (colloquial)	*greenback*
5 cent coin	*nickel*	dollar (colloquial)	*buck*
10 cent coin	*dime*	cashpoint	*automatic teller*

British	American	British	American
aubergine	*eggplant*	biscuit	*cookie*
frankfurter	*frank*	scone	*biscuit*
prawns	*shrimp*	sorbet	*sherbet*
aubergine	*eggplant*	jelly	*jello*
courgette	*zucchini*	jam	*jelly*
maize	*corn*	confectionery	*candy*
chips (potato)	*fries*	spirit	*liquor*
crisps (potato)	*chips*	soft drink	*soda*

British	American	British	American
car	*automobile*	petrol	*gas, gasoline*
bonnet (of car)	*hood*	railway	*railroad, railway*
boot (of car)	*trunk*	tram	*streetcar*
repair	*fix*	underground	*subway*
caravan	*trailer*	platform	*track*
lorry	*truck*	buffer	*bumper*
motorway	*freeway*	single ticket	*one-way ticket*
main road	*highway*	return ticket	*round-trip ticket*

British	American	British	American
shop	*store*	policeman	*cop*
chemist (shop)	*drugstore*	post	*mail*
cinema	*movies*	post code	*zip code*
pavement	*sidewalk*	ring up, telephone	*call*
subway	*underpass*		
gangway	*aisle*	long-distance call	*trunk call*
toilet	*lavatory*		
trousers	*pants*	autumn	*fall*
nappy	*diaper*	gangway	*aisle*
glasses	*eyeglasses*	pavement	*sidewalk*

INDEX

Acknowledgments
The Automobile Association wishes to thank the following libraries, photographers and associations for their assistance in the preparation of this book.
© DISNEY ENTERPRISES, INC. 18; MARY EVANS 10; RONALD GRANT ARCHIVE 11, 14; ROBERT HARDING 22, ROBERT HOLMES 8a, 31, 44, 62, 63, 64, 67, 87, 88, 89; MRI BANKER'S GUIDE TO FOREIGN CURRENCY 119; PICTURES COLOUR LIBRARY 9b; SPECTRUM COLOUR LIBRARY 27a, 56, 58.
The remaining transparencies are held in the Association's own library (**AA PHOTO LIBRARY**) and were taken by H Harris 15b, 24; R Holmes 2, 6, 7, 8b, 12, 16, 17, 19, 20, 22/3, 25, 26, 35, 36, 38, 39, 40b, 41a, 43, 49, 50, 55, 57, 59, 60, 61, 65, 66, 71a, 71b, 72, 73, 74, 75, 76/7, 81, 82, 83, 84, 85, 86, 90, 91a, 117b, 122a; K Patterson 13, 27b, 33, 34, 37, 40a, 41b, 42, 80a, 91b, 117a, 122b, 122c; B Smith 32; P Wood 1, 5a, 5b, 9a, 15a, 21, 45, 48, 51, 52, 53, 54, 79, 80b.

Author's Acknowledgments
Richard Minnich wishes to thank Mr and Mrs Fred B. Minnich, Ms Karen Hicks, Dr. and Mrs John L. Graves, the Los Angeles branch of the California Film Commission and Mr and Mrs Brian Kaminer for their help with this book.

This book makes reference to various Disney copyrighted characters, trademarks, marks and registered marks owned by The Walt Disney Company and Disney Enterprises, Inc.

Contributors
Revision Management: Apostrophe S Limited **Copy editor:** Larry Dunmire **Page layout:** Design 23
Verifier: Sheila Hawkins **Researcher (Practical Matters):** Colin Follett **Indexer:** Marie Lorimer